The Training of the Twelve:
Discussion and Study Guide
For the Book by A.B. Bruce

By

John L. Musselman

and

Joseph McRae Mellichamp

Thousand Fields Publishing
www.1000fieldspub.com

To

My wife Colleen:

"I love thee to the depth and breadth and height my soul can reach."
(Elizabeth Browning)

John Musselman

and

My wife Peggy:

"When I found the one my heart loves…I held her and would not let her go."
(Song of Solomon 3:4)

Rae Mellichamp

The Training of the Twelve:
Discussion and Study Guide
For the Book by A.B. Bruce

THE TRAINING OF THE TWELVE
Introduction

Alexander Balmain Bruce (1831-1899) was educated in Edinburgh, Scotland, and became a parish minister in the Free Church of Scotland, serving for 16 years in Cardross, Dunbartonshire and Broughty Ferry, Scotland. He published his first book, *The Training of the Twelve*, in 1871. In 1875 he was appointed chair of Apologetics and New Testament Exegesis at the Free Church College in Glasgow (now Trinity College), a position he held until his death in 1899.

The Training of the Twelve is universally held to be the definitive work on the way in which the Lord Jesus prepared His disciples for their eventual roles as His Apostles. Dr. Wilbur M. Smith said of Bruce's work, "… in its field, it has never been equaled....*The Training of the Twelve*…is a learned, suggestive, and most practical study of all our Lord said and did for His twelve apostles." Dr. W. H. Griffith Thomas classified it as "one of the great Christian classics of the nineteenth century." Olan Hendrix says, "In more than twenty years in the ministry, few books have influenced and helped me more." And Howard Hendricks, a well-known professor at Dallas Theological Seminary, remarked to John Musselman on one occasion that he had read the book 39 times!

Perhaps the best recommendation for *The Training of the Twelve* was written in the *Foreword* by Stuart Briscoe, noted author and speaker, "…although I have many hundreds of books in my growing library, all carefully cataloged and filed, shelved and ordered, I have just realized that *The Training of the Twelve* has never been officially included in my library! The reason is simple. Ever since I purchased my copy, years ago, it has stayed either on my desk or at my elbow with a handful of other books which I need to refer to constantly. I just haven't been able to part with it long enough to let my secretary put it in its proper place! On second thought, it is in its proper place right where I can get hold of it quickly. I hope your copy will find such a place in your life and experience."

John Musselman's Experience with *The Training of the Twelve*

When I was a senior at the University of Alabama in 1971-72, a fellow student approached me one day as I was walking across the campus and told me he had been looking for me. He handed me some cassette tapes on "Discipleship" by Howard Hendricks and asked me to listen to them. In that series of tapes, Hendricks mentioned two books that, he said, had changed his life: ***The Training of the Twelve*** and ***Dedication and Leadership*** by Douglas Hyde. I bought copies of both, was greatly challenged by Hyde's book, but found it rough going to read A.B. Bruce because of the antiquated writing style of Bruce's day. After completing about 5 chapters of the book, I gave up.

Several years later, when I was in seminary, I decided to have another go at Bruce's book and finished it. As great a work as it is, I thought to myself, "No lay person will ever be able to read this book." So I continued to use it personally, but never felt impressed to recommend it to anyone else.

When I started the Jackson Institute in 1991, I was meeting with my Board one evening (we were in the process of putting together our discipleship curriculum), and they asked me what I thought was the greatest work ever written on the life of Christ and how He trained the Twelve. I told them, hands down, that it was ***The Training of the Twelve***. None of them had ever heard of it. The more we talked, the more intrigued they were with the idea that we should make available to our disciples the best classical works that were available and Bruce's book was clearly one of the ones we should provide.

After describing to the Board members what a difficult book it was to read, one of the men challenged me to re-write it in modern language. I resisted at first, but then gave in. I began the project in

1992 and completed it three years later. The Jackson Institute now has available the modernized version in four volumes, which can be purchased from our Website: www.tji.org.

The Training of the Twelve is one of the key elements of the discipleship curriculum of the Jackson Institute and in this connection, hundreds of men and women have studied this great classic in small groups. Unquestionably, Bruce's work has changed many, many lives for Christ.

Rae Mellichamp's Experience with *The Training of the Twelve*

I began my teaching career at the University of Alabama in the summer of 1969. That fall my wife, Peggy, and I got involved with the student ministry of Campus Crusade for Christ, and I was asked shortly after that to be the faculty advisor for Crusade. As a part of my duties, I was challenged to join a small group of student leaders of the ministry. John Musselman was one of the men in that group. John and I became friends, but he moved on later that same year after graduation while I pursued my career in academia.

After retiring from the university, my wife and I returned to Atlanta, Georgia, to be closer to family and the Atlanta Airport, as we were traveling frequently in conjunction with our work with the faculty ministry (university professors) of Campus Crusade which we had helped launch in 1980. Imagine our surprise and delight to reconnect with John Musselman about whom we had only heard reports but not seen in twenty-five years!

As we began to get reacquainted, John shared with me about a book which he had just finished updating and which he thought would be useful for Daybreak for Men, a Bible Study group of 40-50 businessmen I was leading. The book? *The Training of the Twelve*. I purchased a copy of Volume 1 and read about two pages before it began to dawn on me, "This is the most insightful and profound material on the life of Jesus and His disciples I have ever read—no comparison! I must teach these principles to my Daybreak men!"

Now, as a university professor for 25 years, I supervised 17 doctoral dissertations and sat on many other dissertation committees. I always told my doctoral students, "You may not write anything for my approval before submitting to me a detailed outline of what you propose to write." And that is how I always taught—graduate students and undergraduates alike—from detailed outlines. So when I began teaching the principles of *The Training of the Twelve* to the men in my Bible Study, I developed a set of detailed outlines for each of the 53 chapters in the book. And these outlines form the basis of this Study Guide. My suggestion to you is to use the Study Guide side-by-side with the book. Read through a section of the guide to understand what is coming in the book, then read the book, and finally answer the discussion questions.

Bruce's book has had a profound influence on my own life as a disciple of Jesus, and, I believe, it has had a similar impact on the lives of many men and women whom I've had the privilege of teaching over the last twenty years.

THE TRAINING OF THE TWELVE
1. Beginnings

Scripture

John 1:29-51

Obscure Events?

- John's Prolog. John 1:1-18
- John's introduction to Jesus.

Five men [Andrew, John (the son of Zebedee), Peter, Philip, and Nathaniel] were becoming acquainted with Jesus and were putting their faith in Him, and they were subsequently giving their full attention to Him, becoming Apostles of the Christian faith.

- These events are not mentioned in the other gospels.
- Why were these events so important to John?

John the Baptist

- His origin.
- His Message.
  - "Repent for the Kingdom of Heaven is at hand."
  - "Make ready the way of the Lord."
- His Disciples—Andrew and John (the son of Zebedee)
  - Were looking for the Messiah.
  - Would leave John to follow Jesus.

The Character of the Five

- They were waiting for the One who would fulfill God's promises.
- They were men who hungered for righteousness unlike that of the Pharisees.

Simon Peter

- Jesus saw who Simon Peter was.
- Jesus saw who Simon Peter could be.

Philip

- He was assured of who Jesus was.
- He wanted others to know who Jesus was.

Nathanael

[Identified elsewhere as Bartholomew]

- He was a man of moral excellence.
- He was a man of humility.

The Belief of the Five

- They knew Jesus' offices.
  - The Lamb of God. John 1:36
  - The Christ. John 1:41
  - The Messiah. John 1:45
  - The Son of God. John 1:49
  - The King of Israel. John 1:49
- They had John's (the Baptist) testimony.
- They had their impression of Jesus.

Questions

1. Is Jesus Christ your Savior and Lord?
2. At this stage of your life, what are you pursuing—what has your heart?
3. Would you say you are hungering and thirsting after real righteousness? Is knowing God your greatest desire?

4. John describes the character of the men who ultimately became Jesus' Apostles. What would you say are some of your strongest character traits?
5. Apart from the Holy Spirit's work in our lives, we cannot have godly character. What character traits would you ask the Holy Spirit to develop in your life?
6. Would you be willing to ask the Lord to help with deficiencies of character and to conform you more and more to His image?
7. What do you need to do this week in response to the things God has shown you from this study?
8. Do you believe that God will allow you to see greater things than you now see about Him and His kingdom? Why or why not?

THE TRAINING OF THE TWELVE
2. Fishers of Men

Scripture

Matthew 4:18-22; Mark 1:16-20; Luke 5:1-11

Stages in Fellowship with Jesus

- They accompanied Him when it was convenient.
- They were with Him most of the time.
- They were chosen by Him from among His followers.
  [As a means of carrying on the work of the kingdom.]

The Apostles

- Their Background.
  - Humble birth.
  - Inferior social status.
  - Low paying occupations.
  - Bereft of education.
  - Lacked interaction.

- Their Qualifications.
  - As messengers for a universal religion.
    - Free from Jewish narrowness.
    - Compassion for the world.
  - As messengers for a spiritual religion.
    - Emancipated from regulations.
    - Embraced noble and heroic ideas about human and divine dignity.
    - Willing to personally bear a cross.

The Spiritual Condition of the Twelve

- Overall: lacking.
- Specifically: immature. Luke 5:4-8

- Dread of the supernatural.
- Morbid fear of God.

One Grand Virtue

- They were captivated by a dream about a kingdom.
- They were united by their attachment to Jesus.
- They were drawn by the action of their Master.

They were animated by their devotion to Jesus and to the divine kingdom which made them capable of any sacrifice.

Questions

1. The Twelve went through three stages of development in their relationship with Jesus. At which stage would you say you are in your relationship with Him?
2. What experiences have brought you to your present spiritual condition?
3. Jesus trained the Apostles and gave them duties. What do you believe your duties ought to be [are] in the kingdom?
4. What qualifications do you believe a follower of Christ ought to have in order to be effective for Him?
5. What bad things do you personally need to unlearn before you can become an effective follower of Christ?
6. Do you possess the "one grand distinguishing virtue" that the early disciples had? If not, how do you think you can attain it?
7. Could you be charged with having a heart full of compassion for the kingdom of God with Jesus of Nazareth as its King?
8. In order to follow Jesus today, all we have to do is forsake our sins. Are you still holding on to any sins that you are unwilling to forsake? If so, will you deal with them now?

THE TRAINING OF THE TWELVE
3. Matthew the Publican

Scripture

Matthew 9:9-13; Mark 2:13-17; Luke 5:27-32

Selection Criteria of Jesus

- Disregard for worldly wisdom.
- Focus on the heart—spiritual fitness.
- Disregard for history/external associations.
- Concern for all nations and all time.

Matthew's Name

- "Matthew" in his gospel.
- "Levi" in Mark and Luke.

Matthew's Occupation

- Tax collector.
- Publican.

The Time of Matthew's Call

- Matthew 9:9: Full account of the Sermon on the Mount.
- Luke 6:13-17: Places Matthew at the scene of the Sermon.

Matthew's Call

[Abrupt or considered?]

- Shared hometown.
- Knowledge of Jesus.
- Witness of miracles.

Matthew's Repentance

- Many tax collectors were guilty of fraud and extortion.
- Matthew was probably delighted to become a burden lifter rather than a burden imposer.
- The significance of his feast:
  - Emancipation from:
    - Drudgery.
    - Incompatible relationships.
    - Sin.
  - An act of worship.
  - A farewell party.
  - An introduction of Jesus.
  - A scandal. Luke 5:30

The Great Physician

Answers Jesus gave for spending time with publicans and sinners.

- The *professional* argument. I go to the places where sinners are because I am a Physician.
- The *political* argument. It is good policy to be the friend of sinners who have much to be forgiven.
- The *natural* argument. It is natural to seek the lost. There is great joy in finding things that were lost.

Questions

1. Early on in your study of the Life of Christ, it is essential that you become aware of the issues that Jesus considers to be of utmost importance. The following questions will bring you to the heart of the issues raised in the chapter. They are hard questions (Jesus never seemed to ask easy ones). Open your heart and look deeply. Don't be afraid of what you will find there. He can cleanse you of all that resides in the darkest corners of your heart.

7

a. Are you in any way prejudiced against any group or race of people that God has created in His image?
b. You've just learned that a close friend of yours has committed adultery or stolen some money from the office. How would you respond to him or her? How would Jesus respond?
c. You've been invited to share your testimony with 300 inmates in a major prison. What are your thoughts?
   - They deserve to be there. Let them stay forever. How could they have committed those crimes?
   - I will go and speak, but I want to keep my distance from them.
   - Will I be safe?
   - What good will it do? After all, they are hardened?
   - I am no different from them. I am a sinner saved by grace and these are the kind of people with whom my Lord associated. I will go with the purpose of seeking to win them for Christ, and to build up those who already know Him.

2. A.B. Bruce maintains that the Pharisees were very inhumane, full of pride, prejudice, harshness and hatred. Do any of these adjectives apply to you?

3. Have you ever gotten "dirty" for the cause of Christ? Have you ever spent time ministering to someone who was unlovely, unkempt, morally questionable? Consider sharing your experience with the others in your group.

4. Is there any area of your life for which Jesus would rebuke you for being "religious"?

5. The Pharisees had no power over Jesus. In fact Bruce says, "…it never discouraged Him. He went calmly on His way doing His work." Will you risk being a true disciple of Christ by offering yourself to Him as one who will associate with anyone for the cause of the Kingdom, and not be concerned about what someone else may say?

6. Are you ashamed of the gospel?

THE TRAINING OF THE TWELVE
4. The Twelve

Scripture

Matthew 10:1-4; Mark 3:13-19; Luke 6:12-16; Acts 1:13

The Ministry of Jesus

- The first period.
  - He worked alone.
  - His teaching was elementary.
  - His miracles were geographically confined.
- The second period.
  - The work had to be divided and shared.
  - His teaching was deeper and more complex.
  - His activities were geographically dispersed.

The Purpose of the Twelve

- To be apprentices.
- To become His agents.
- To learn:
  - What they should do.
  - What they should believe.
  - What they should teach.

The Time of His Selection

- In relation to Passover. John 6:4
- In relation to the Galilean mission. Matthew 10:1
- In relation to the Sermon on the Mount.
  - Luke 6:13,17
  - Mark 3:13-15

The Number of Apostles

- Symbolic meaning.
    - Twelve tribes.
    - Messianic King.
- Mystical meaning.
  Twelve Thrones

The Twelve Apostles

- First group.
    - Simon Peter, the man of rock
    - Andrew, Peter's brother
    - James, son of Zebedee (son of Thunder)
    - John, son of Zebedee (son of Thunder)
- Second group.
    - Philip, the earnest inquirer
    - Bartholomew (Nathaniel), the guileless Israelite
    - Thomas (Didymus), the Twin
    - Matthew, the publican (tax collector)
- Third group.
    - James (the Less), the son of Alphaeus
    - Thaddaeus (Judas or Jude) possibly the son of James and grandson of Zebedee
    - Simon the Zealot
    - Judas of Kerioth, the traitor

Why They Were Chosen

- Externals.
    - Poor, illiterate Galilean rustics.
    - His own relatives (James, John, Jude)
    - Devoid of social status.
- Internals.
    - Simple, sincere, energetic Galileans.
    - Humble, not proud.
    - Devoted to Him.

\- Spiritually qualified.

The Wisdom of His Choices

- It does not take a *great* man to be a *good* witness.
- Two or three prominent men in twelve is a good ratio.
- Christ was their hero; their sole desire was to tell about Him.

Questions

1. When the time comes for you to begin discipling others, what traits would you look for before making your choices?
2. Would you be willing to disciple someone you would not normally be drawn to in a social setting? Why or why not?
3. If you were to begin discipling others right now, what would they be able learn from you about walking with Christ?
4. Jesus preferred devoted men rather than men of worldly stature or learning. Why is it so important to find devoted people to disciple?
5. Jesus trained twelve men and turned the world upside down. Can you explain how this astounding work took place?
6. What application does question #5 have for you as you become more involved in fulfilling the Great Commission (Matthew 28:18-20)?

THE TRAINING OF THE TWELVE
5. Hearing and Seeing

Scripture

Luke 1:1-4; Matthew 13:16,17; Luke 10:23,24; Matthew 5:7; Luke 6:17-49; Matthew 13:1-52; Matthew 8:16,17; Mark 4:33,34

Assignments

- The Apostles needed to see and hear the facts of an unparalleled life—the life of Jesus.
- This would be necessary if people were to believe their story.
  - "What we have seen and heard..." 1 John 1:3
  - "Having carefully investigated..." Luke 1:3

The Doctrine of the Kingdom

- The Great Sermon.
  - The character of the citizens. (Beatitudes)
  - The joy of the Kingdom. (Blessed)
  - The righteousness of the Kingdom (Pharisees)
  - The ethics of the Kingdom. (Love)
  - The religion of the Kingdom. (Love of God)
  - The character of the Kingdom. (Within the heart)
- The Parables of the Kingdom.
  - The Sower. (Responses)
  - The Tares and the Net. (Good and evil)
  - The Treasure and the Pearl. (Importance of the Kingdom)
  - The Mustard Seed and the Leaven. (Growth of the Kingdom)
  - The Grain. (Growth of the Kingdom in Stages)

Note. Until Jesus appeared, no one had ever used earthly things to symbolize heavenly things.

The Philanthropic Work of the Kingdom

- The extent of His miracles.
    - One Sabbath. Mark 1:32-34
    - Multitudes. Mark 3:20
- The response to His miracles.
    - The religious leaders. Mark 3:22
    - His family. Mark 3:21
    - The recipients. Matthew 9:8
    - The Twelve.
- Matthew. Matthew 8:17
- John. John 20:31

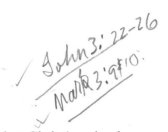

John 3: 22-26
Mark 3: 9'10.

Note. The Apostles marveled not at the fact that Christ's miracles were supernatural; they were amazed at the unfathomable depth of divine compassion. The love of Christ remained for them throughout their lives a thing that surpassed knowledge!

Questions

1. How do we see and hear the words and works of Jesus today? *scriptures*
2. In what ways have you seen the mighty hand of God move recently? *already*
3. What kind of kingdom do you expect the Lord to establish? *Not yet.* Are your ideals in line with what Jesus taught? *- games*
4. Do you believe the Lord can still do "wonderful works"? Why or why not?
5. In what ways are you currently seeking to build Christ's Kingdom?

Jer 21:25

Babie — Heart mods.

John Steels bus

13

THE TRAINING OF THE TWELVE
6. Lessons on Prayer

Scripture

Matthew 6:5-13; 7:7-11; Luke 11:1-13;18:1-5

The Necessity of Prayer

- Jesus was a man of prayer.
  - Mark 1:35.
  - Luke 6:12.
  - Matthew 14:23.
- Jesus often taught about prayer.
  - He gave a model. Matthew 6:5-13
  - He advocated persistence. Luke 11:1-13; 18:1-5
  - He required agreement. Matthew 18:15
  - He challenged expectancy. John 16:23,24
- Jesus encouraged the disciples in prayer.
  - To make it their habit.
  - To learn about waiting.

A Model for Prayer

- The Lord's Prayer. Matthew 6:5-13
  - A formula, an outline.
  - Six petitions.
    - Three refer to God's glory.
    - Three to man's good.
  - In His name. John 16:24
- The Lord's expectations.
  - It was a temporary solution.
    - The symptom—lack of words.
    - The problem—lack of faith.
  - They should pray as He prayed. John 17

His Teaching on Prayer

- Bold—choice of illustrations.
  - The evil father.
  - The unrighteous judge.
- Warm—sympathetic to our wrong thoughts about God.
- Wise.
  - Avoids teaching a "philosophy of waiting".
  - Assure that desires will be fulfilled.

His Reasoning about Prayer

- Inspires hope in God—even in the darkest hour.
- Demonstrates the impossibility of an uncaring God. Luke 11:9

Questions

1. Reflect on your own prayer life. Has it become a vital part of your spiritual life? Explain. *yes*
2. What aspect of prayer do you struggle with the most (listening, praise, waiting on God, thanksgiving)? *Making time*
3. What aspect of prayer brings you the most joy? *Praise*
4. When and over what issues are you most apt to give up on in prayer? *day - day issues*
5. Is there anything that you used to pray for that you have stopped praying for because you have lost hope that God will act upon it? *No.*
6. Do you seek first the Kingdom of God (Matthew 6:33), or do you mostly pray for things you want God to provide or do for you? *Latter*
7. What have you learned from this chapter that could transform your prayer life and draw you closer to God?

15

THE TRAINING OF THE TWELVE
7. Lessons in Religious Liberty—Fasting

Scripture

Matthew 9:14-17; Mark 2:16-22; Luke 5:33-39

Principles for Life

- Jesus' simple approach to living.
  - A disregard for insignificant mechanical rules.
  - A dependence on principles of morality and piety.
- Jesus' departure from current practices.
  - Fasting.
  - Ceremonial purifications.
  - Sabbath-keeping.
- Consequences for the Christian.
  - Beginnings of a great moral and religious revolution.
  - Deliverance of the church from the Moasic ordinances.
- Consequences for the Twelve.
  - Their conduct was called into question.
  - They were personally censured.
  - Jesus shielded them from assault.

Fasting

- General Requirements.
  - Annually on the Day of Atonement. Leviticus 23:27-29
  - Four fasts in the 4th, 5th, 7th, and 10th months. Zechariah 8:19
  - Bi-weekly on Mondays and Thursdays. Extra-Biblical sources
- Practice of the Pharisees.
  - Zealous and frequent.
  - Pretentious, hypocritical, and rote.
- Practice of John and his disciples.
  - Zealous and frequent.

- Simple, sincere, and morally earnest.
- Practice of Jesus and his disciples.
  - Jesus fasted for 40 days to start His ministry. Matthew 4; Luke 4
  - Otherwise, He and His disciples did not fast.
- Questions from John's disciples.
  - Motivated by surprise.
  - Desire for instruction.

Principles for Fasting

- Three Parables.
  - The groom.
  - Patches.
  - Wineskins
- One Guideline.
  - Fasting should be done when:
    - There is great crisis.
    - There is great question.
  - Otherwise fasting is:
    - Forced.
    - Unnatural.
- One Principle.
  In all voluntary religious service, where we are free to regulate our own conduct, the outward acts should be made to correspond to the inner motives of the heart.
- Two reactions.
  - Religious ways don't change.
  - Christianity is counterfeit.
- Jesus' response.
  - Preference to old ways is natural.
  - Acceptance of new ways is prudent.

Questions

1. If Jesus' disciples needed to be set free from the "bondage of the Mosaic ordinances," and "from the aggravating bondage of

an empty way of life that had been passed down as traditions from the Jewish fathers," from what do modern day Christians need to be set free?

2. From what religious duties or customs does the modern day church need to be set free? From what religious duties or customs do you need to be set free?

3. Why should one not engage in spiritual duties in a mechanical way? Do you ever offend in this way?

4. Do you understand the need to fast? Do you ever practice this spiritual discipline in your own life?

5. Are you open to "new wine" in your life or are you unwaveringly committed to traditional ways of doing things? If you have a "conservative mind" and have an "inadequate conception of the vital force of belief," what do you need to change in order to strengthen your faith?

6. Are you personally ready to put off the trappings of religion to have a more vital relationship with Jesus?

Thoughts on todays duties.
. License vs. Freedom
. Martha vs. Mary in terms of having to go to all church functions
• Formal vs. informaldness,
. Forms of worship.
. Music

18

THE TRAINING OF THE TWELVE
8. Lessons in Religious Liberty—Ritual Washing

Scripture

Mark 7:1-23; Luke 11:37-41

The Charge

- Pharisees from Jerusalem. "Why don't Your disciples …"
- Pharisee at dinner. "His host was amazed to see …"
  At issue here is what is preeminent in our lives:
- The traditions of men.
- The commands of God.

Rabbinical Commands

- The goal: Ceremonial purity—cleansing from any impurity that may have come from contact with:
  - A Gentile.
  - An unclean Jew.
  - An animal.
  - A body or body part.
- The burden: Ritual washing.
  - The hands.
  - Cooking and eating utensils.
- An example—a story from the Talmud.
  - Rabbi Akiba.
  - Rabbi Joshua.

Jesus' Defense

- His tone.
  - With the disciples of John.
  - With the Pharisees.

- The principle.
  "The careful observance of human traditions leads, without fail, to a corresponding neglect and corruption of the eternal laws of God."
- Fools and hypocrites.
  - A fool is one who is incapable of discerning between what is vital and what is not in morals.
  - A hypocrite is one who replaces the weightier matters (justice, mercy, faith) with the trivial ones (washing the hands, paying a tithe of herbs).
- His arguments.
  - Scripture. "This people honors Me ..."
  - An illustration: The fifth commandment.
    - God's command. "Honor your father and mother ..."
    - Man's tradition. Pledged to God—Corban
  - Encouraged neglect of morality.
  - Promoted fraud and hypocrisy.

True Defilement

- Instruction for the crowd.
- Explanation for the disciples.
  - Eating with unwashed hands is OK.
  - Living with an evil, unrenewed heart is not.

The Result

- Ceremonialism is abolished.
- Eternal laws are elevated.

Questions

1. What are some ways today that Christians place religious tradition over the moral law of God?
2. Is there anything inherently wrong with the following religious functions?
   a. Going to church on Sunday.

b. Early morning quiet time.

c. Tithing.

d. Memorizing Scripture.

e. Serving the poor.

g. Going on a two-week mission trip.

h. Holding an office in church.

3. At what point would doing any of these things merit Jesus' rebuke?

4. Have you gotten into a "religious rut" (i.e., doing things that look good outwardly, but not inwardly)?

5. What are you currently doing for God that is not motivated by a sincere love for God? In other words, are there any areas of your life where you are performing for God or others (like family, friends, pastor, etc.), but inside you know you are dead spiritually?

6. Have you or do you use your freedom in Christ to justify your lifestyle when you know it is in opposition to the moral law of God?

7. What are some of the areas of your life that you need to look at after reading this chapter?

THE TRAINING OF THE TWELVE
9. Lessons in Religious Liberty—Sabbath Observance

Scripture

Matthew 12:1-14; Mark 2:23-3:6; Luke 6:1-11; 13:10-16; 14:1-6; John 5:1-18; 9:13-17

The Charge

- Jesus' observance of the Sabbath was the most frequent point of criticism.
- The Crime: Performing works of healing on the Sabbath.
- The Accusers: Pharisees looking for faults.
- The Offense: Jesus was breaking the petty rules the religious leaders had devised to improve observance of the Sabbath.

The Wisdom of Jesus

- His Defense. He does not call into question the obligation to keep the Sabbath.
- His Positions.
    - On fasting. Fasting is voluntary, people should fast as they are inclined.
    - On washing. Washing should be neglected in favor of sincere inward purity.
    - On the Sabbath. All *rules* for observing the Sabbath should be examined in light of the underlying *principle* of the Sabbath.

The Key to His Teaching

- Purpose of the Sabbath. It was a holiday given by a merciful God to His subjects.
- Sabbath Observance.
    - What is best for man's spiritual and physical well-being?

- The day should be kept in a spirit of thankfulness to God for His gracious consideration.

Two Great Uses of the Sabbath

- Rest for the Body.
    - Excludes absolute inaction.
    - Includes:
        - Acts of necessity.
        - Acts of mercy.
- Worship of the Spirit.
    - Excludes burdensome religious duties.
    - Excludes mechanical, legal service.

Sources of Jesus' Proofs

- Historical.
    - The case of David. 1 Samuel 21:6
    - The principle: Necessity has no law.
- Common Practice.
    - The practice of the priests.
    - The principle: To do well on the Sabbath.
- Providence.
    - The Father works on the Sabbath.
    - The Son also must work on the Sabbath.
        - Works of humanity.
        - Works of mercy.

Lord of the Sabbath

- The Sabbath: Burden or Benefit?
    - Burden. Jesus would have done away with it.
    - Benefit. Jesus is the best judge of observance.
- The Sabbath: Saturday or Sunday?
    - Saturday. Commemorates the creation.
    - Sunday. Commemorates the resurrection.

Questions

1. How do you keep the Lord's day? How do you rest? How do you worship?
2. Are there any changes you need to make in your practice?
3. Is the Sabbath a joy to you to which you look forward or is it a burden?
4. What are some works of necessity or mercy in which you could engage on the Sabbath?
5. This last question has to do with the "necessary virtue" (the power to bear isolation and its consequences") that Christ was trying to teach the Apostles as He addressed the Pharisees (on fasting, ceremonial washings, and Sabbath observance). Give one illustration from your life about how you have been able to stand alone for the Lord Jesus Christ in the face of opposition. If you do not have one, perhaps this is the time in your life to seriously ask Him to make you courageous and bold.

THE TRAINING OF THE TWELVE
10. First Attempts at Evangelism—The Mission

Scripture

Matthew 10; Mark 6:7-13; 30-32; Luke 9:1-11

The Objective

- The masses were like shepherdless sheep.
- The mission was to meet their spiritual needs.

The Sphere Assigned

- Restricted to villages and hamlets of Galilee.
- Excluded larger towns and cities.
- Focused exclusively on the Jews.
  - Excluded Gentiles.
  - Excluded Samaritans.
- Reasons for restrictions.
  - Their hearts were too narrow.
  - Their prejudices were too strong.
  - Their character was:
    - Too Jewish.
    - Too little Christian.
  - They were lacking:
    - God's grace.
    - God's Spirit.

The Nature of the Work

- Unlimited Healing Powers.
  - No need for restrictions—save pride.
  - The motive for miracles—Christ's will.
- Restricted Preaching Prerogatives.
  - Repentance of sin.

25

[At this stage, the disciples understood nothing of the doctrine of the cross.]
-   Readiness for the Kingdom. The coming not the character. [There was danger of misunderstanding the nature of the Kingdom.]

Results of the Mission

- The Works Achieved Notoriety.
    -   With the masses.
    -   With the political leaders.
- The spiritual impact was:
    -   Fleeting.
    -   Superficial.
    -   The compassion of Jesus was unabated.

"A great deal noise and tumult, confusion and uproar, darkness mixed with light, and evil with good, is always to be expected in the beginning of something very glorious in the state of things in human society or the church of god." Jonathan Edwards

- There were now two movements underway:
    -   Awakening the masses.
    -   Training the committed.

The Assessment of the Master

We may infer three cautions from Jesus' assessment upon the return of the Seventy:
- "Rejoice that your names are recorded…"
- "Come away by yourselves and rest."
- Usefulness does not imply goodness—Judas.

The outcome: He impressed on His disciples a large-hearted, generous concern for the spiritual well-being of the people.

Questions

1. Do you believe that you must be fully equipped and trained before the Lord can use you in someone else's life? *No.*
2. Have you been trained to share the Gospel? If not, would you like to be? *Yes.*
3. What should be your motivation for witnessing? *obedience,*
4. Do you see the importance of evangelizing the masses and training the few? In which of these two groups do you see yourself? *Both.*
5. Do you understand how your own personal spiritual health can *yes* be injured while you are seeking the salvation of others? If your spiritual life is unhealthy now, what could you do to *No.* restore it?
6. Far too many Christians have very little, if any, compassion for people who are lost in their sins. If this is true of you, would you be willing to faithfully pray that God would give you a genuine burden for souls? (You would receive enormous help in this area by reading Charles Spurgeon's book, *The Soul Winner.*)

THE TRAINING OF THE TWELVE
11. First Attempts at Evangelism—The Instructions

Scripture

Matthew 10; Mark 6:7-13; 30-32; Luke 9:1-11

Overview

- Two Parts.
  - "Care Not." What they were to do as apprentices.
  - "Fear Not." What they were to do and endure as Apostles.
- Two Timeframes.
  - The present. Small geographically-limited beginnings.
  - The future. Great, world-wide undertakings.
- One Motive. Reassurance.

Instructions for the Present. Matthew 10:5-15

- Responsibility of apprentices.
  - Cast aside worry.
  - Rely on the Master.
- Provisions for apprentices.
  - Buy nothing.
  - Take nothing.
    - Money.
    - Knapsack.
    - Clothing.
    - Sandals.
    - Staff.
- Summary: "Go at once, and go as you are, and do not concern yourself with food or clothing, or anything you need for your body. Trust God for these."
- Assumption: "Jesus took it for granted that they would find in every place they went at least one good man with a warm heart who would welcome the messengers of the kingdom to house and table because of his pure love of God and for truth."

Instructions for the Future. Matthew 10:16-31

- Precautions for Apostles.
    - Serpents—cunning.
    - Doves—simplicity.
- Virtues of Apostles.
    - Caution. To avoid being cut off prematurely or unnecessarily.
    - Faithfulness. To complete God's work and fight for truth.
- Behavior of Apostles.
    - Before tribunals:
        - Don't be anxious.
        - Speak the truth.
    - Before ignorant people (mobs):
        - Avoid where possible.
        - Speak the truth.
- Prediction for Apostles.
    - Result: persecution.
    - Remedy: flee.
    - Rationale: servants and the Master.
- Encouragement for Apostles.
    - Those who can kill the body.
    - He who can destroy the soul.

Questions

1. With the command "care not" in mind, what are some specific ways in which God has provided for you in the past?
2. Have you learned the lesson of trusting God for the necessities of life, even when things get tight?
3. Would you be willing to confess your lack of trust or confidence in His ability to take care of you in a specific area where you are concerned? If so, why not take some time right now and talk with the Lord about your worries? Ask Him to free you from the bondage of anxiety and worry.
4. What does living by faith mean to you? Do you live by faith?

5. How does it impact you when you think about the fact that kingdom work is not always pleasant? Does it make you want to retreat?
6. Do you exhibit the virtues of caution and fidelity when you are exposed to danger?
7. What is the most dangerous situation you have ever encountered for the sake of Christ?
8. Are you willing to endure more dangers and hardships for His sake?
9. Where can you find safety when you encounter dangers of any kind?
10. How can you behave more like a dove and a serpent?
11. Are you afraid to die? If so, how are you coping and dealing with it so it will not paralyze you from doing all that He has for you to do?
12. Granted, this first missionary sermon by our Lord is a high mountain. In broad terms, how has this chapter affected you and your calling to become a Disciple Maker?

THE TRAINING OF THE TWELVE
12. The Galilean Crisis—The Miracle

Scripture

John 6:1-15, Matthew 14:13-21; Mark 6:33-44; Luke 9:11-17

The Miracle Itself

- Location.
  - Bethsaida, Peter and Andrew's town.
  - Bethsaida Julius, another location.
- Participants.
  - Source of information.
  - Reliability of information.
- Authenticity.
  - 5000 witnesses.
  - Consistency of accounts.
- Uniqueness.
  - Five barley loaves, two fish.
  - No sufficient reason. 5000/4000
    - Duration of meetings.
    - Proximity of villages.
  - Motivation: compassion.

A Critical Miracle. (Didactic. *To Teach*)

- Symbolic.
  - It provided a text for a subsequent sermon.
  - "I am the bread of life (for your soul).
- Discriminating.
  - To the spiritual, it demonstrates who He is.
  - To the carnal, it simply filled their stomachs.

Mercy and Judgment

- The case for mercy.

31

- The crowd needed food.
- The crowd was large!
- The case for judgment.
  - The need to sift.
    - To dispel false hopes.
    - To clarify the nature of His kingdom.
  - The timing of sifting.
    - Excitement from miracles—maximum exposure.
    - Proximity to Passover—maximum symbolism.
  - The strategy for sifting
    - The disciple's plan.
    - Jesus' plan.

Results of the Miracle

- Impact on the crowd.
  - They wanted to make Jesus their King.
  - They would revolt against King Herod.
- Impact on Jesus and the Twelve.
  - Jesus sent the Twelve away.
  - Jesus withdrew from them.

Questions

1. The most important question you could ask yourself after reading this chapter is the one A.B. Bruce poses in the last paragraph: "Why do I profess Christianity?" Here are some possibilities:
    a. Because you are following some custom or tradition.
    b. Because it improves or enhances your reputation.
    c. Because it gives you some worldly advantage, perhaps in business.
    d. Because of your sincere faith in Jesus Christ as your Savior and Lord.
    e. Why do you follow Christ?

2. Have you come to the place in your life where you will follow Jesus no matter what the cost?
3. Do you follow Him for who He is, or for what He can do for you?

THE TRAINING OF THE TWELVE
13. The Galilean Crisis—The Storm

Scripture

Matthew 14:24-33; Mark 6:45-52; John 6:16-21

The Situation

- Location—Sea of Galilee
  - Size. Approximately 13 miles by 8 miles.
  - Elevation. 700 feet below sea level.
  - Setting. West of the Golan Heights (2700 feet).
- Scenario—Disaster for the Twelve.
  - Heading to Bethsaida.
    - Matthew 14:22, Mark 6:45
    - John 6:16,17
  - Facing the storm.
    - Another storm. Mark 4:35-41
    - This storm. Was it preventable?

The Storm as a Symbol

- It Happened at Night.
  - During the fourth watch. 3:00 to 6:00 a.m.
  - Sudden and violent.
  - Fatigue, terror and despair.
- Jesus Was Absent.
  - Where was He?
  - What was He doing?
- All Progress Stopped.
  - Straining against the wind.
  - Three or four miles.

Lessons in Faith

- It Prepared Them:

- For the future.
- For His permanent absence.
- It Gave Them Confidence.
  - In His leadership.
  - In His love and care.
- Parallels Between the Storm and the Crucifixion
  - They didn't expect to see Jesus.
  - They were terrified when they did.

Peter on the Water

- Peter's Proposal.
  - Generous and enthusiastic.
  - Rash and inconsiderate.
- Jesus' Response.
  - Humored the impulse.
  - Intended to teach.
- Peter's Nature.
  - Bold when there was no danger.
  - Fold when there was a trial.

Questions

1. To date, what is the greatest trial or test of faith you have experienced?
2. Reflect on these questions as they relate to that trial.
   a. What danger did you face with the trial?
   b. Describe the darkness. Did you lose hope? Were you in despair?
   c. Did you hold your own or did you go backwards?
   d. Where was Jesus?
   e. What lessons did you learn from the trial?
   f. Did you see the weakness of your faith during the trial?
3. Will it be possible for you to remain strong in the faith the next time you experience a trial?
4. How can you prepare for trials?

THE TRAINING OF THE TWELVE
14. The Galilean Crisis—The Sermon

Scripture

John 6:24-58

The Situation

- Time.
  - Immediately after feeding the 5000.
  - Several months before the Passover.
- Place.
  - Capernaum.
  - Synagogue.
- The Mood of the Crowd.
  - Expectant. John 6:14-15
  - Exuberant. John 6:22-24
- The Mood of Jesus.
  - He knew the crowd. John 2:24-25
  - He was reflective. John 6:15
  - He closed ranks.
- Important Symbolism. John 6:32-33
  - Bread—Manna.
    - From heaven.
    - For Israel.
    - For 1 or 2 days.
  - True Bread—Jesus.
    - From heaven.
    - For the world.
    - For eternity.

What True Bread Is

- "I am the bread of life."
- One of the seven "I am" claims.
- Spoke of the incarnation.

- Foretold His sacrificial death.
  (Bread must be broken)

What True Bread Does

- It gives eternal life. John 6:35
- It enables resurrection. John 6:44
- It destroys death. John 6:49-50
  Thus, it deals with physical as well as moral corruption.

How the True Bread Is Appropriated

- Eating and drinking signify belief. John 6:35
- Transubstantiation/Consubstantiation.
- Three truths:
  - The sermon refers to the death of Christ.
    (So does the Lord's Table)
  - The sermon stands alone.
    (From the sacrament)
  - The sermon establishes faith.
    (For salvation)

How the Sermon Was Received

- They grumbled. John 6:41-42,52
- They deserted. John 6:66.
- The Twelve remained. John 6:68-70

Questions

1. Have you personally feasted upon Christ, the bread of life?
2. Why is it important to continually partake of His flesh (to live by faith)?
3. What ought to be our response to the Savior who came down from heaven so we could live forever with Him?

4. Have you any doubts about the certainty of your immortality?
5. What does communion mean to you?

THE TRAINING OF THE TWELVE
15. The Galilean Crisis—The Sifting

Scripture

John 6:66-71

Rejection

- His Response.
    - He was grieved by it.
    - He desired it.
- His Rationale—True Disciples.
    - God given. John 6:37
    - God drawn. John 6:44
    - God taught. John 6:45
- The Crowd's Reaction.
    - The excuse—the hardness of the teaching.
    - The reason—the offense of the teacher.
- The Twelve's Response.
    - Their experience.
        - A strange sermon.
        - A serious dispersion.
    - The question. John 6:67
    - The expectation.
        - Of the Eleven.
        - Of the one.
    - Three Anchors.
        - What enabled the Eleven to ride out the storm?
        - What will enable you to ride out storms?

The First Anchor—Religious Earnestness

- Their Desire: The Words of Eternal Life.
- Their Concern:
    - Heavenly food for the soul, not
    - Perishable food for the stomach.

39

- Their Goal:
  - A place in His Kingdom, not
  - Better worldly circumstances.

The Second Anchor—The Alternatives

- The Actual Choices:
  - Stay with Jesus.
  - [Go back to John.]
  - Go with the Pharisees.
  - Go with the Sadducees.
  - Go with the Crowd.
    - Stupidity.
    - Indifference.
- The Philosophical Choices:
  - Christianity.
  - Atheism/Legalism.
    - Purely ethical.
    - Character admiration.
  - Pantheism.
  - Naturalism.

The Third Anchor—His Character

- They Had Enjoyed His Fellowship.
- They Had Witnessed His Miracles.
- They Had Followed His Guidance.
- They Had Become His Friends.

Questions

1. The message of this chapter is, without a doubt, one of the most important we have encountered to date. It fully acknowledges the darkness, deceptiveness, and secretive nature of the human heart and warns against following the Lord Jesus Christ for any other reason except that the person is "God-given, God-drawn, and God-taught." Examine your own heart and ask yourself

40

this question, "Will you follow Jesus wherever He leads even if it means suffering, pain, or personal loss?"

2. Can you identify ways you have been disappointed or disillusioned with God? Does this reflect a wrong idea about who Jesus is or what He came to do?

3. Was there ever a time when you became so disillusioned with God that you either abandoned Him for a time or were tempted to abandon Him?

4. What anchors do you think you need in order to be steadfast when the storms of opposition come against your faith in Christ?

5. Do you want to be faithful to the end? Do you think you will be able? What will it take in order to "make it"?

THE TRAINING OF THE TWELVE
16. The Leaven of the Pharisees and the Sadducees

Scripture

Matthew 16:1-12; Mark 8:10-21

Background

- Recent Itinerary.
  - Tyre and Sidon.
  - Ten Cities (Decapolis).
- Recent Event.
  - 5000 people.
  - 7 loaves, a few fish.
  - 7 large baskets.
- Current Itinerary.
  - Dalmanutha.
  - Magadan.
- Current Event.
  - Pharisees' [, Sadducees'] Request.
    - A sign from heaven,
      - Unique and startling.
      - Signifying God's power
    - Not an earthly healing.
      - Routine and ordinary.
      - Possibly from the Devil.
  - Jesus' Rebuke
    - Wicked. They rejected Him.
    - Adulterous. They rejected God.

Watch Out!

- A New Tack.
  - Back in the boat.
  - To the other side.

- A New Threat.
  - Pharisees.
    - Zealous.
    - Strict in morals.
    - Exclusively Jewish.
    - Hypocritical.
  - Sadducees.
    - Moderate.
    - Lenient in morals.
    - Openly Pagan.
    - Materialistic.
      - Political orientation: Herodians.
      - Cultural orientation: Philosophers.

Pharisees, Sadducees and Herodians were all worldly-minded. They opposed Jesus because He was not of this world.

The Radical Vice

- Ungodliness.
  - Blind to truth.
  - Dead to God.
- Leaven.
  - A constant craving for evidence.
  - A continuing spread of corruption.
- The Cure.
  - A new heart.
  - A willing spirit.

The Disciples Misunderstand

- A Natural Conclusion.
  - They were removed.
  - They were negligent.

✓ • The Master's Message.
  - Their abundant concern—material things.
  - Their limited concern—spiritual things.

Questions

1. All around us are evidences that Jesus Christ and His kingdom of grace are upon us. What are some of those evidences?
2. Those who are spiritually blind and have a dead heart are in need of a sign. If we are not asking God for signs, for what should we be asking Him? *Faith*
3. Do you have unbelief or doubts, that is, do you have a difficult time believing the promises of God about salvation, heaven, provision, protection, etc?
4. Would you be willing right now to go to God in prayer and confess whatever unbelief has held you in bondage and ask Him to give you freedom to trust Him implicitly?
5. Material things preoccupied the minds of the disciples. They should have been more focused on the things of God and His interests. Could this be said of you? Are you focused more on the everyday things of life or on the things of Christ?
6. Jesus warned the disciples, "Beware of the leaven of the Pharisees and Sadducees." What might He be warning you about today?

1. Church, good in bad places,
2. Faith.
3. At times.
4. Yes.
5. Yes, often.
6.

THE TRAINING OF THE TWELVE
17. Peter's Confession

Scripture

Matthew 16:13-20; Mark 8:27-30; Luke 9:18-21

Background

- Geography. *Greek*
  - Caesarea.
  - Caesarea Philippi.
    - The name.
    - The attractions.
- The Question.
  - His motivation.
    - Not for Himself.
    - For the Twelve.
  - The controversy.
    - Seriousness or levity.
    - Prejudice or sincerity.
    - Decision or indecision.
    - Intelligently or ignorantly.

The Opinions about Jesus

- The Peoples' Opinion.
  - A Prophet.
    - Relation to the Messiah—John the Baptist.
    - Resemblance to the Prophets.
      - His tenderness—Jeremiah.
      - His sternness—Elijah.
      - His teaching—Ezekiel or Daniel.
  - Greater than a Prophet.
    - His works.
    - His teaching.

45

- His character.
- The Religious Leaders' Opinion.
  - Their labels.
    - Samaritan.
    - Illegitimate.
    - Glutton, drunkard.
    - Blasphemer.
    - Companion of sinners.
  - Their conclusion.
    - A demon.
    - The Devil.

The Report of the Twelve

- Assessment of Opinion.
  - He did not react.
  - He did not accept.
- The Spokesman—Peter.
  - "You are the Christ."
  - "The Son of the Living God."
- Jesus' Response.
  - He did not correct Peter.
  - He praised Peter.

Peter's Confession

- Two Propositions.
  - Jesus was the Messiah.
  - Jesus was divine (God).
- Two Different Views.
  - The Messiah expected by the Jews was simply a [superior] man.
  - The Messiah who came was fully human and fully divine.

Jesus' Response to Peter

- The Source.
  - Not humanly discernible—from Peter.
  - Divine utterance—from the Holy Spirit.
- The Message.
  - Peter's *faith*, not his person is the message.
  - The "keys of the kingdom" is this *doctrine*.
  - This *confession* is the foundation of the church.

"You Simon Barjonas, are Petros, a man of rock, worthy of your name Peter, because you have made that bold, good confession; and on the truth you have now confessed, as a rock, will I build My church; and as long as it abides on that foundation it will stand firm against all the powers of hell."

Questions

1. What do others around think about Jesus? What do they say about Him?
2. Do you personally believe that Jesus was the Messiah? Do you believe He was the Son of God, that is, God the Son?
3. In what specific ways has your profession of faith changed your life (behaviors, speech, attitudes, thinking patterns, lifestyle, commitments, etc.)?
4. How can your profession of faith in Christ as the divine Messiah render you unassailable against the powers of Hell?

THE TRAINING OF THE TWELVE
18. First Lesson on the Cross: First Announcement of Christ's Death

Scripture

Matthew 16:21-28; Mark 8:31-38; Luke 9:22-27

Background

- Before Caesarea Philippi.
    - A temple destroyed. John 2:19
    - A serpent raised. John 3:14
    - A bridegroom separated. Matthew 9:15
    - Flesh and blood given. John 6
    - The sign of Jonah. Matthew 16:4
- At Caesarea Philippi.
    - Signs of the times.
        - Work in the provinces.
        - Mood in the capitol.
    - Reassurance for the Apostles.
        - Necessary preparation.
        - Mature faith.
    "It was only after Jesus heard Peter's confession that He was satisfied that the strength necessary for enduring the trial had been attained."
- After Caesarea Philippi.
    - He must go to Jerusalem.
        - A public place.
        - A judicial process.
        - In full view.
        - In the place of sacrifices.
    - And suffer many things.
        - This was painful for the Twelve.
        - This was scandalous to the Twelve.
    - From the leaders.
        - The priests made the suggestion.

- - The scribes invented the grounds.
  - The elders (Sanhedrin) imposed sentence.
- And be killed.
  - The fact is stated.
  - The details are omitted.
- Be raised up on the third day.
  - Impossible.
  - Improbable.
  - Timely.

Peter's Rebuke

- His Behavior.
  - He is irreverent and disrespectful.
  - He contradicts.
  - He tries to bully.
- His Character.
  - Presumption.
  - Too free and intimate.
  - Self-will.
- Contrasts.
  - Inspiration.
    - The Holy Spirit.
    - Flesh and Blood.
  - Names.
    - A rock.
    - A stumbling block.
- The Rebuke.
  - Jesus likened Peter to Satan.
    - The Prince of the World. Self interest rules the world.
    - The Accuser of the Brethren. He holds that believers have no higher motive.

"All people are selfish at heart, and have their price. Some may hold out longer than others, but when pushed to the limits, every person will prefer his things to the things of God. A man will give all that he has for his life. His moral integrity and his piety are not exempt. This is Satan's creed."

- Peter questioned Jesus as did Satan.
  - "If You are the Son of God …" Luke 4:3
  - "If You are the Son of God …" Luke 4:9

"The severe language spoken by Jesus on this occasion shows in a pointed way that He literally had a holy hatred for everything that smacked of self-seeking."

Questions

1. The simplest statement of the Gospel is: "Christ died for me." Can you see what He had to go through in order to go to the cross for you?
2. This lesson focuses on the self-interest of Peter. How can self-interest overpower duty (the cause of God) in your life?
3. Satan believes that in the final analysis, every person will prefer his own things to the things of God. Is this true of you?
4. How can you ensure that you will not be an instrument in the hands of Satan, that you will not prefer safety to righteousness?
5. Jesus abhors all self-seeking. Will you commit yourself now—and every day—to seek first His kingdom? It is the only way to win your heavenly Father's approval.

THE TRAINING OF THE TWELVE
19. First Lesson on the Cross: Cross-Bearing the Law of Discipleship

Scripture

Matthew 16:24-28; Mark 8:34-38; Luke 9:23-27

Background

- Two Announcements.
  - "I must be put to death."
  - "You must bear a cross."
- Two Audiences.
  - First announcement.
    To the Twelve.
  - Second announcement.
    - To the Twelve.
    - To all believers.

    "By this announcement, the King and Head of the church proclaims a universal law which is binding on all His subjects: *all who are in fellowship with Him are required to bear a cross.*"
- Some Responses.
  - What does Jesus have to do with crosses?
    - Isn't He exempt?
    - What advantage is divinity?
    - Is the Master not better than the servant?
  - What do we have to do with crosses?
    - Didn't Jesus take our place?
    - Why should we bear a cross?
  - The universal law applied.
    - He suffered for righteousness sake.
    - The godly suffer in an evil world.

    "Only those willing to be crucified with Him would be saved by His death. A person's willingness to bear a cross

51

is indispensable to right understanding of the doctrine of salvation through Him."

The Meaning of the Cross

- Its Significance.
  - The penalty of death.
  - The troubles of the godly.
- For the Twelve.
- For Believers.
  - Untrue characterizations.
  - Unrealized ambitions.
  - Isolation and loneliness.

Reasons for the Law of the Cross

- Two Lives/One Choice. Matthew 16:25
  - The natural life.
  - The spiritual life.
  "He is no fool who gives up that which he cannot keep to gain that which he cannot lose." Jim Elliott
- The Value of the Soul. Matthew 16:26
  - The soul for the world? Exchange
  - The world for the soul? Redemption
  "The great ambition of millions of people is to be happy [personal peace and affluence] rather than to be blessed by being saved, noble-minded, and sanctified."
- The Second Coming.
  - Cross bearers will receive a crown of righteousness.
  - Those who avoided the cross everlasting shame and contempt.
  "Christians do not need to be afraid that they are using Christ for their own ends if they seek to become virtuous."

Questions

1. What cross or crosses have you had to bear for faithfully following Christ?
2. What was your initial response to this trial or difficulty?
3. Over time, how did you adjust your thinking about your cross? Did you come to accept it? Are you mad at God?
4. Is there anything in your life today that would indicate you are seeking the natural life as opposed to the spiritual or sacrificial life?
5. How could your thinking and attitudes about suffering and cross-bearing change to reflect the teachings and example of Jesus?
6. Are you faithfully seeking to follow and serve Jesus regardless of the consequences in personal suffering?

THE TRAINING OF THE TWELVE
20. The Transfiguration

Scripture

Matthew 17:1-13; Mark 9:2-13; Luke 9:28-36

Background

- What Happened?
  - Heaven came to earth.
  - Jesus was transformed.
  - Moses and Elijah appeared.
  - A voice came forth.
- When Was It?
  - Matthew. "Six days later."
  - Mark. "Six days later."
  - Luke. "Eight days later."
- After What?
  - Peter's confession.
  - Mention of His death.
  - Comments on the cross.

"While the previous communications and sermons about the cross were fresh in the thoughts of all the people, the wonderful events we are now writing about took place."

Jesus, Moses, Elijah

- The Contrasts.
  - Moses.
    - Represented the Law.
    - Departed life peacefully. Deuteronomy 32:49
  - Elijah.
    - Represented the Prophets.
    - Translated in a chariot. 2 Kings 2:11

- Jesus.
  - Fulfilled the Law and the Prophets.
  - Crucified on a cross.

"And behold, two men were talking with Him; and they were Moses and Elijah, who, appearing in glory, were speaking of His departure which He was about to accomplish in Jerusalem." Luke 9:30,31

- The Disciples (Peter, James, John).
  - On the mountain.
  - In the garden.

"[The Master took these disciples with Him] ... so He might not be totally without company and warm sympathy as He walked through the valley of the shadow of death, and felt the horror and the loneliness of the situation."

Why the Transfiguration?

- Comfort for Jesus?
  - From the Twelve?
  - From the people?
  - From the leaders?
- Comfort for Jesus.
  - A foretaste of glory.
  - Affirmation of heaven.
    - "Lost sheep." Luke 15:7
    - "Little ones." Matthew 18:10
  - Approval of the Father.

The Voice from Heaven

- At His Baptism.
- At the Transfiguration.
- At His Crucifixion.

"These voices were for His encouragement and strengthening, and expressed the Father's quiet satisfaction over His humiliation and obedience unto death."

The Lesson for Christians

- Peter's Reaction.
  - His mindset.
  - His desire.
- Our Admonition—Listen to Jesus Speak.
  - About His death.
  - About cross-bearing.
    - Don't give in to the flesh.
    - Don't lay aside burdens.
    - Don't withdraw from trials.
    - Do your part like a man.

"Even the loving redeemer of mankind felt tempted to be weary in well-doing—weary of encountering the opposition from sinners and of putting up with the spiritual weakness of the disciples."

Questions

1. Do you have a clear understanding of what Jesus did for you on the cross? The words below describe some of the benefits that are bestowed on each of God's children. Test yourself by giving a brief definition or explanation of the following terms that have to do with the theology of His death. (Check yourself by using a Bible dictionary or dictionary of theology.)
   a. Redemption.
   b. Propitiation. *Removing anger.*
   c. Reconciliation. *Brought back*
   d. Forgiveness. *Don't hold it against*
   e. Expiation. *Satis Taking away guilt.*
   f. Justification. *Do david with love*
2. What can we expect for our heavenly Father to provide for us when we are experiencing severe trials? How does He encourage and comfort you when you suffer?

56

3. Since cross-bearing is a duty required of all disciples, how do you need to change your thinking about the teaching of Jesus on this subject?
4. A.B. Bruce says that you should "do your part like a man" as it pertains to working in God's kingdom while you are on earth—and in due time you will have a house that is eternal in the heavens. What do you think he means when he says "do your part like a man"?

THE TRAINING OF THE TWELVE
21. Training In Character: Discourse on Humility
As This Little Child

Scripture

Matthew 18:1-14; Mark 9:33-37, 42-50; Luke 9:46-48

Background

- The Setting.
  - After the Transfiguration.
  - In Galilee.
  - After speaking of His impending death.
  - In Capernaum.
- The Motivating Dream.
  - The Cross, or
  - The Crown?
- The Burning Question.
  - Peter, James and John.
  - The others.
  - Who is the greatest?
- The Master's Task.
  - To engender loyalty and submission.
  - To instill the law of love in relationships.
  - To remove pride, ambition, jealousy, and envy.

"It was the most important task Jesus had to perform with the Twelve, for what good could these men do as ministers of the kingdom as long as their main concern was about their own place in it?"

The First Lesson He Taught

- Become as a Little Child.
  - Unpretentious.
    - A natural characteristic.

- Unconcerned with rank.
  - Unambitious.
    - Unconcerned with their place in the kingdom.
    - Yielded in simplicity to the Master.
- Become as Jesus.
  - He is the perfect example of humility (forgetting self).
  - He thought only of the Father's glory and man's good.
  - He did not desire, nor did He receive, honor from men.
  - He did not come to be served, but to serve.
  - He humbled Himself to become the least:
    - A child born in a stable.
    - A man of sorrows.
    - A Savior on a cross.

"Being childlike, as He demonstrated, is an inevitable characteristic of those who are growing spiritually. The absence of this trait is the mark of moral immaturity. The little person, even when he has good intentions, is always thinking about consequences, always scheming. He is forever thinking about himself, his honor, dignity, reputation—even when he says he is doing good."

The Second Lesson He Taught

- Receive Little Ones.
  - The weak, the insignificant, the helpless
  - The humble in spirit.
  - Those of little influence or importance.
- Treat Them Well.
  - Graciously and lovingly.
  - Without giving offense.
    - By harshness.
    - By heartlessness.
    - By demeaning them.

"Harshness and contemptuousness are vices that cannot be separated from an ambitious spirit. An ambitious man is not necessarily cruel in his outward appearance. But he can be capable of making heartless plans in cold blood."

The Third Lesson He Taught

- The Nature of Heaven.
- The Nature of Salvation.

"If the Son of Man provided care for the lost, the humble, and for those who were morally bankrupt, how much more would He care for those who are simply little! ... The love of the Son of Man, in the eyes of all true disciples, surrounds the meanest and the vilest in the human race with a halo of sacredness."

Questions

1. Are you an ambitious person?
2. If so, in what ways did this lesson speak to you about being ambitious?
3. Do you become jealous toward others who in some way have more than you—whether position, authority, money, home, automobile, etc?
4. If so, in what ways did this lesson speak to you about being jealous?
5. The key issue which Jesus addressed with the Twelve in this discourse had to do with being self-willed, self-seeking. What have you learned from the lesson that will help you live as Christ did—with meekness, humility and love?
6. How can you—and should you—become like a child?

THE TRAINING OF THE TWELVE
22. Training in Character: Discourse on Humility
Church Discipline

Scripture

Matthew 18:15-20

Background

- His Desire for the Church.
  - Holy.
  - Loving.
  - United.
- His Directions for the Church.
  - For its purity.
  - For its peace.
  - For its well-being.
- His Guidelines for the Apostles.
  - Binding and loosing.
  - Inflicting and removing [church censures].
  "The offender who remains unrepentant is not to have religious fellowship with the one he offended, nor with anyone in the church."
- His Illustrative Examples.
  - Gentiles were excluded from the Temple.
  - Tax-gatherers were excluded from fellowship.
- His Targeted Offenses.
  - Private, personal [against individuals].
  - Public, scandalous [against the church].

The Process

- The Order.
  - Confront in strict privacy.
  - Confront with witnesses.
  - Bring before the church.

- The Outcome.
  - Makes confession easy.
  - Avoids the shame of exposure.
  - Requires pure and holy motives.
  - Precludes scandal and gossip.
  - Minimizes resentment of offended.
  - Discourages the nosy and overzealous

"It is characteristic of the loving spirit of Jesus, the Head of the church, that He is horrified at the possibility that anyone who is a believer could become like a Gentile or tax-collector to other believers."

Strictness and Love

- Members.
  - The church on earth.
  - The church in heaven.
- Mercy.
  - To the members.
  - To the offenders.
    - By providing a foretaste of hell.
    - By enlisting the prayers of believers.

Multiplying Members

- The Objective.
  - Morality?
  - Members?
- The Promise.
- The Conditions.
  - Two or more.
  - Agreement.

"He did not want His church to consist of a collection of clubs which do not have communion with one another, any more then He desired it to be a monster hotel which receives and boards all who come without any questions being asked. He did not make the promise we are now considering to stimulate sectarianism. Rather, He wanted to encourage people to cultivate values which have always been rare on earth—brotherly kindness, meekness, and love. The thing He values, in a word is not the shortage of numbers, due to the lack of love. He values, instead, the union of hearts in humble love among the greatest number possible."

Questions

1. Is there any sin in your life that, if it were known, would make you a candidate for church discipline? If so, are you willing to forsake it and allow someone to hold you accountable so you will not fall back into it again?
2. Are you challenged to be on guard against every form of sin and to strive to live a holy life for the honor and glory of your Savior, Jesus Christ? What actions do you need to take today to strengthen yourself spiritually against the temptations of the world, the flesh, and the devil?
3. Are there any brothers or sisters in Christ whom you know are no longer living for Him? Would you be willing to go to them (after prayer) with the intent of restoring them to fellowship with the Lord?
4. Are you willing to do everything in your power in your church to promote its purity as well as its peace?

THE TRAINING OF THE TWELVE
23. Training in Character: Discourse on Humility
Forgiving Injuries

Scripture

Matthew 18:21-35

Background

- Discourses on Humility.
  - As this little child.
  - Church discipline.
  - Forgiving injuries.
- Peter's Question.
  - Demonstrated intelligent attention.
  - Showed conscientious obedience.
  - Revealed true relationship.
- Jesus' Response.
  - Dealt with Peter's pride.
  - Revealed the breadth of his charity.
    - Puny.
    - Insignificant.
  "Jesus' response tells those who desire to be like God that they must multiply their pardons: 'I do not say to you up to seven times, but seventy times seven.'"
- Jesus' Illustration.
  (par´a-b'l, Gr. parabolé, *likeness*), derived from the Greek verb parábállo, composed of the preposition *para* meaning *beside* and the verb *bállo, to cast*. A parable is thus a side by side comparison of two objects for the purpose of teaching.

Object in the Parable	Object in Reality
- First Transaction.	
• Creditor	God
• Debtor	Sinner

- Second Transaction
  - Creditor   Believers
  - Debtor   Other
                         believers

The Two Debts

- Magnitude.
  - 10,000 Talents. $20,000,000
  - 100 Denarii. $40
- Realism.
  - The first debtor—a person of high rank.
  - The second debtor—a person like us.
- Contrasts.
  - The first debtor.
    - Preoccupied with position.
    - Unconcerned with faithfulness.
    - Interested in personal benefit.
  - The disciples.
    - Motivated by ambition.
    - Argued over who was the greatest.
    - Desired a place of distinction.

"This is a paraphrase of what Jesus said to them: 'Look at what the men do who long to be great! They rob their king of his revenue, abuse the opportunities that are theirs because of their position, and make themselves rich. And while they create scandals by neglecting their own obligations, it is in their character to demand an exact payment from any little one who may have innocently become their debtor—not by fraud, but by misfortune.'"

The Two Creditors

- The King.
  - Is slow to anger.
  - Displays great kindness.
  - Gives time to repent.

- Accepts promises to change.

"He does not treat us as our sins deserve or repay us according to our iniquities." Psalm 103:10

- The Unmerciful Servant.
  - Truly deserved punishment.
  - Had no resources to repay.
  - Was totally self-absorbed.
  - Was incredibly inhuman.

Judgment Pronounced

- Universal Application.
  - None exempt.
  - None favored.
- Judicially Appropriate.
  - "My heavenly Father."
  - The merciful Son.

"'See to it, then, that you forgive every person of their trespasses—really forgive, not just pretend to forgive. Forgive from your very hearts.' Jesus educated His disciples with severe plainness in His speech so they could truly be great in His kingdom—great, not in pride, pretension, and presumption, but in loyal obedience to the commands of their King, especially to this law of forgiveness."

Questions

1. Is there any one whom you have not forgiven? Ask the Lord to reveal to you anyone whom you may have overlooked.
2. Will you forgive them, no matter how severe the offense?
3. When will you forgive them? Do you need to go to someone and talk to them about an offense they have committed against you?
4. What do you suppose happens when we follow this law of forgiveness? What happens to us? What happens to the party who offended us?

THE TRAINING OF THE TWELVE
24. Training in Character: Discourse on Humility
The Temple Tax

Scripture

Matthew 17:24-27

Background

- The Sequence.
    - The Transfiguration.
    - The Argument.
    - The Tax Collectors.
    - The Sermon.
- The Story?
    - Matthew's predilection.
    - Jesus' modus operandi.
- The Illustration.
    - A testimony of poverty.
    - A demonstration of humility.
        - He didn't plead poverty.
        - He didn't ask exemption.
- The Response.
    - He consents to be treated commonly.
    - He desires to live peacefully.
    - He complies with their laws.

"The greatest in the kingdom—Jesus—is an example of the humility that He imparted to His disciples. He shows them by His own example their need to express holy and loving concern to avoid giving offense, not only to Christians, but even to those who are unbelievers."

Jesus and the Law

- The Tax. Exodus 30:11-16

- Purpose.
- Application.
- The Argument. About Who is Greatest
  - Sermon motivation.
  - False conclusions.
    - Jesus argued against paying.
    - This was not humiliation.
- The Reality.
  - The Son learned obedience.
  - The Son came to serve.
  - The Son was subject to the law.
    - He was circumcised.
    - He worshipped at the Temple.
    - He offered sacrifices.
    - He attended the feasts.
- The Lessons.
  - For Him to pay was humiliating and incongruous.
  - For Him to pay was not to be expected.
  - For Him to become a man was not to be expected.
  - For Him this was an act of voluntary humiliation.

In effect, He said to them, "If I were like you, longing to receive honors, and determined to assert My importance, I would stand on My dignity and arrogantly reply to these tax collectors. 'Why do you bother Me about temple dues? Do you not know who I am? I am the Christ, the Son of the living God. The Temple is My Father's house. And I, His Son, am free from all obligations that servant's have.' But carefully note that I do nothing of the kind. ... I am conscious of who I am; I know from whence I came; I know where I am going. With all this abiding deep in my soul, I submit to be treated as a mere common Jew. I will allow My honors to be postponed. I will not make any demands for recognition that is not voluntarily granted. ... If the rulers knew who I was, they would be ashamed to ask Me to give temple dues. But since they do not, I accept and bear all the wrongs that are the result of their ignorance."

- The Provision.
  - His Instructions.
    - As Lord over nature.
    - As Sovereign over all.
  - His Miracle.
    - Was not for his benefit.
    - Did not diminish his humiliation.
    - Was offered as an object lesson.

Giving and Receiving Offenses

- The Reason.
  - To avoid giving offense in this instance.
  - To address giving and receiving offences generally.

  "He was about to speak to them mostly on the subject of giving and receiving offenses. And He wanted them, and especially their key man (Peter), first of all to observe how very careful He was not to offend."
- His Humility.
  - Nothing is said of His being offended.
  - He did not take offense at the request.
  - He was not offended that they did not know Him.
  - He gave without complaining.
  - He was careful not to give offense.

  "What was His purpose in coming to the world? What was His constant work after He came, but to cancel offenses and to put an end to enmities—to reconcile sinful men to God and to each other? ... How many offenses could have been prevented if the conciliatory spirit of the Lord always controlled those who are called by His name?"

Questions

1. What do you understand humility to be?
2. Are you willing to live a life of voluntary humiliation? What would this mean for you personally?

3. Are there any petty disputes or offenses that have not been cleared up between you and someone else? If so, are you willing to seek reconciliation?
4. How can you live your life so that you try to avoid giving offense to others?
5. What can and will you do to bring unity and peace in the body of Christ?
6. Will you ask the Lord to help you become a peace-maker for the glory of His name?

THE TRAINING OF THE TWELVE
25. Training In Character: Discourse on Humility
The Interdicted Exorcist

Scripture

Mark 9:38-41; Luke 9:49,50

Background

- The Sequence.
  - The Transfiguration.
  - The Discussion.
  - The Child.
  - The Confession.
- The Apostle of Love?
  - John's recollection.
  - John's involvement.
  - John's temperament.
    - Calling down fire.
    - Sitting on the right.

"[At this time], he is committed to Jesus with his mind, and is tender and intense in his attachment to Him. But he is also bigoted, intolerant, and ambitious."

- The Apostle of Love.
  - The fruit of the Spirit.
  - The growth of the years.

An External Test Only

- The Exorcist.
  - What we know about him.
    - He was doing a good work.
    - He had a high regard for Jesus.
  - What we infer about him.
    - He was honest and sincere.
    - He wanted to imitate the Twelve.

- He may have been spiritually superior.
- He may have been a local prophet.
- The Test.
  - External qualifier: One of the Twelve.
    - Type 1 Error: Judas.
    - Type II Error: Nicodemas.
  - Internal qualifiers: Character qualities.
    - Humility.
    - Loyalty.
    - Devotion.

Mixed Motives

- The Prohibition.
  - Based on doubt.
    - Honest hesitation.
    - Deserves consideration.
  - Based on jealousy.
    - They desired a monopoly.
    - They would be gatekeepers.
- Their Motivation.
  - In the case of the Argument: Pride.
  - In the case of the Exorcist. Pride
- Pride and Arrogance.
  - "Ours is the only true church of Christ."
  - "Our beliefs are the only true way."

"We believe the consciences of the Twelve were of the honest kind, because they were willing to be instructed. They told their Master what they had done, so they could learn from Him, whether it was right or wrong. People whose conscience is a sham do not behave this way."

Jesus' Counsel

- The Rule. The most important matter in spiritual character is the bias of the heart.

- Two Cases:
  - "If the heart of a man is with Me, he is really for Me—even though he seems to be against Me because he doesn't know any better, or because he made an honest mistake, or because he is not a part of the group of those who have declared they are My friends."
  - "If a man is not with Me in his heart (the case of the Pharisees), then he is really against Me—even though he seems to be on God's side (and therefore on Mine) because of his orthodoxy and zeal."

Applications for the Church

- Beware of hasty conclusions about the spiritual condition of others when those conclusions are based only on outward appearances.
- Many things in history would have been different if Christ's mind had dwelt more in those who were called by His name.
- All efforts at reconciliation deserve our warmest sympathies and prayers.

Questions

1. After reading and studying this section, what has the Lord taught you today about judging others? *Be careful.*
2. Do you deal with any of the following? Pride? Jealousy? Intolerance? Judgmental spirit? *Yes at times.*
3. Are you hasty to make conclusions about the spiritual condition of others by observing only external factors in their lives? If so, how can you avoid this practice? *Sometimes,*
4. What should be your attitude toward those who belong to another denomination? Should we love the whole Christian body more than any part? *Yes.*
5. How can you be a part of bringing about unity and love in the body of Christ? *Prayer.*

Phil. 1:18
Mat. 11:30

THE TRAINING OF THE TWELVE
26. The Sons of Thunder

Scripture

Luke 9:51-56

Background

- The Journey.
  - Leaving Galilee.
  - Traversing Samaria.
  - Judea beyond the Jordan.
    - Geographical direction.
    - Frame of mind
- The Story?
  - Luke the author.
    - Companion of Paul.
    - Evangelist to Gentiles.
  - Luke' purpose.
    - Continuation of interdicted exorcist.
    - All-inclusive nature of Christianity.

"This current incident, like the one just before it, shows a striking contrast between the harsh spirit of the disciples and the gentle, gracious spirit of their Master."

A Closer Look at John

- John's Participation.
  - At the well. John 4
  - In the village. Luke 9
  - In many villages. Acts 8:14,25
- John's Growth.
  - Spiritually green.
    - Opinionated.
    - Judgmental.

- Demanding.
- Intolerant.
- Zealous.
  - Spiritually Mature.
    - Apostle of salvation.
    - Apostle of love.
- John's Extremes.
  - Intense love.
    - Jesus.
    - Believers.
  - Intense hate.
    - Hypocrisy.
    - Apostasy.
    - Half-heartedness.
- The Disciple Jesus Loved?
  - Jesus loves us for what we can become.
  - John was absolutely devoted to Jesus.

The Cruel Proposal

- What it was not.
  - A sudden outburst of anger.
    - For hospitality refused.
    - By weary, irritated men.
  - A display of race-related hatred.
    - The Samaritans were racially mixed.
    - The Apostles were racially pure.
- What it was.
  - Jealousy for the honor of the Lord.
  - Reaction to the insult of their Master.

The Samaritans

- A Mixed Race.
  - Heathen Assyrians.
  - Degenerate Jews.

- Blasphemous Heretics.
  - They rejected the Scripture.
  - They worshiped at Gerizim.
  - They dishonored Jesus.

Jesus' Response

- In General.
  - Gentle.
    - Unenlightened Samaritans.
    - All who do not know who they worship.
  - Thunderbolts.
    - Those who should but did not know better. Pharisees
    - Powerful, privileged, presumptuous sinners. Religious
- In Particular.
  - James and John. Luke 9:55
    - Fleshly passion.
    - Self-will, pride.
  - All Disciples. John 4:35
    - Messengers of mercy.
    - People of all nations.
  - For Himself.

Questions

1. What are ways in which you express anger to others?
   a. Words.
   b. Passive/aggressive behavior (seething, sulking, silent treatment, etc.).
   c. Overt behavior (revenge, getting even).
   d. Other.
2. In your life, what needs to be tempered by the light of wisdom and softened by the heat of love?
3. Do you measure others by what they are, or by what they can become?

4. If James and John, Apostles of our Lord, were capable of this, do you think you also are capable of committing gross sins? What is the only answer to our sin problem?

5. Is it possible for Christians to be jealous for the honor of their Lord, but propose actions for dealing with situations that are contrary to His will?

6. Jesus drove the money-changers out of the Temple motivated by righteous anger. What are some ways Christians can express righteous indignation and please the Lord?

7. What changes in character need to take place in your life so you could be more effective in reaching people with the gospel?

8. What is the significance of Christ's death for you as it pertains to your character?

THE TRAINING OF THE TWELVE
27. The Doctrine of Self-Sacrifice:
Counsels of Perfection

Scripture

Matthew 19:1-26; Mark 10:1-27; Luke 18:15-27, John 10:39-40

Background

- The Setting.
  - Leaving Galilee.
  - Judea beyond the Jordan.
- The Significance.
  - His baptism.
    - "The Lamb of God." John 1:29
    - The Holy Spirit. Mark 1:9-11
  - His first disciples.
    - "The Lamb of God." John 1:36
    - Follow Me. John 1:39

"We believe His journey to the Jordan was a pilgrimage to holy ground on which He could not set His foot without feeling profound emotions. ... And these memories urged Him on to the grand consummation of His life's work. He had been charged by His baptism, His vows, the descent of the Holy Spirit, and the voice from heaven, to crown His labors of love by drinking from the cup of suffering and death for man's redemption."

New Lessons for the Twelve

- Sacrifice for the Sake of the Kingdom.
  - Appropriate for the place.
  - Appropriate for the time.
  - Appropriate for the mood.
- Two Interviews.
  - With the Pharisees. Matthew 19:3-12

78

- With the young ruler. Matthew 19:16-26
- Two Topics.
  - Abstaining from marriage.
  - Renouncing property.

Sympathy for Celibacy

- Principle for Divorce.
  - Justified by marital infidelity.
    - Adultery.
    - Desertion. [1 Corinthians 7:15]
  - Not allowed for:
    - Incompatibility.
    - Drifting apart.
    - Different habits.
    - Different religions.
    - Obnoxious relatives.
- Rationale for Celibacy.
  - The disciples' question.
  - The teacher's response.
    - Congenital conditions.
    - Societal impositions.
    - Personal choices.

Personal Property

- The Young Ruler's Situation.
  - Outwardly: desired eternal life.
  - Inwardly: loved possessions.
- The Teacher's Response.
  - Forsake inordinate love of money.
  - This forsaking is very difficult.

"For if a man's life on earth does not consist totally of possessions and family relations, at least they occupy a very prominent place. … Did Jesus then, frown or look down on these things as unfavorable to, if not incompatible with, the interests of the divine kingdom and the longings of its citizens?"

The Early Church's Position on Celibacy and Voluntary Poverty

- "From a very early period, the church entertained the idea that Jesus meant to teach the inherent superiority of a life of celibacy and voluntary poverty over that of a married man possessing property."
- "They [celibacy and poverty] were not necessary for salvation—that is, to obtain a simple admission to heaven—but they were necessary to obtain an *abundant* entrance"
- "So while these virtues of abstinence were not to be demanded of everyone, they were to be commended as **counsels of perfection** to those who were not content to be commonplace Christians."

Four Fatal Errors

- Abstaining from things that are lawful is a higher sort of virtue than moderation.
- Christ's teaching simply states that *in certain cases* celibacy and voluntary poverty are superior to marriage and wealth.
- If abstinence is a higher virtue than moderation, it should be required, not optional.
- If consistently applied, celibacy and voluntary poverty would result in the destruction of society and the end of the human race.

The Little Children

Questions

1. We learned in this chapter that Jesus went back to visit the place of His baptism. Think about a time in your life when God did a special work in your life. Perhaps you can recall your

conversion experience when you first came to know Jesus Christ as your Lord and Savior. Or maybe you remember a time when you realized God called you to do a special work for Him. Times of recommitment and rededication to Him are also treasured memories.

Think about a time when God did a special work in your life. Mentally go back and try to remember the lesson you learned and apply it to your present circumstances.

2. How does your marriage enhance your work in Christ's kingdom?
3. How does your marriage detract from your work in Christ's kingdom?
4. How do your possessions enhance your work in Christ's kingdom?
5. How do your possessions detract from your work in Christ's kingdom?
6. What are some specific ways you can apply the principle of moderation in your life?

THE TRAINING OF THE TWELVE
28. The Doctrine of Self-Sacrifice:
The Rewards

Scripture

Matthew 19:27-30; Mark 10:28-31; Luke 18:28-30

Background

- The Setting.
  - Region of Judea.
  - East of the Jordan.
- The Questions.
  - Pharisees—Divorce?
  - Young Ruler—Eternal Life?
  - His Disciples—Who?
  - Peter—Rewards?
- The Case.
  - We have done what the young man could not do.
  - We have done what rich men find hard to do.
  - We have left everything to follow You.
  "Jesus gives a full reply to Peter's question. It is full of encouragement and also issues a warning for the Twelve, and for all who profess to be servants of God."
- The Answer.
  - Great rewards.
  - Right motive.
  - A parable.
- In General.
  - Rewards vs. sacrifices.
  - Generous exaggeration.
  - Proper recompense.
  "Having an earnestness that was full of passion, and speaking a word that was full of tender, grateful feeling, He promised them thrones as if they had been fairly earned! If we believed them, these great and precious promises would make

sacrificing easy. Who would not part with a fishing boat for a throne?"

Rewards for the Twelve

- Thrones in this Lifetime.
    - [In a restored kingdom of Israel?]
    - As founders of the Christian church.
    - As permanent Apostles of the church.
    - As architects of Christian doctrine.
- Thrones in Eternity.
    - As rulers of the Twelve tribes of the true Israel.
    - As those who receive honor in the kingdom of God.

Rewards for Believers

- Rewards in this Lifetime.
    - Return in Kind.
        - To individuals.
        - To generations.

"Multitudes of God's servants have had what the world would say are miserable lives. Does the promise, then, simply and absolutely fail in their case? No. For ... there are more ways than one in which it can be fulfilled. For example, blessings can be multiplied by a factor of a hundred without their external size being altered. ... Fathers and mothers, and all earthly friends, become unspeakably dear to our hearts when we have learned to say: 'Christ is first, and everyone else must be second.'"

    - Power.
        - Of enjoyment.
        - Of feeling.
        - To love.
    - Joy.
- Rewards in Eternity: Eternal Life.

Illustrations

"Such are the rewards that are provided for those who make sacrifices for Christ's sake. Their sacrifices are only seeds that are sown in tears. Afterwards they reap an abundant harvest in joy"

Questions

1. Up to this point in your life, what are some of the sacrifices you have made for the sake of the kingdom of Christ?
2. From the lesson, do you see the importance of making sacrifices for Christ? Why do you think it is important? What does it accomplish?
3. Have you ever read a promise from Scripture, then experienced a difficulty or hardship in life, and said in your heart, "O Lord, You have deceived me!"? As a disciple of Jesus Christ, how did you handle the apparent discrepancy between the written word and your personal experience?
4. A.B. Bruce tells us that if "only we could lay a firm hold on the blessed hope that is set before us here," we would be transformed into "moral heroes." Do you believe this is true? If you focused more on heaven and the fact that you will be held morally accountable for the life you have lived here on earth, would you live any differently? If so, how?
5. How have you been rewarded in this life for sacrifices you have made for the kingdom?
6. How is the value of something you sacrifice increased?
7. While you were studying these passages and reading A.B. Bruce's commentary on them, did the Lord speak to you about anything specific that He wanted you to sacrifice for Him? How are you presently responding to His request?
8. What new insights have you learned about making sacrifices for the Lord?

THE TRAINING OF THE TWELVE
29. The Doctrine of Self-Sacrifice:
The First Last and the Last First

Scripture

Matthew 19:30; 20:1-20; Mark 10:31

Matthew Henry

Background

- The Setting.
  - Region of Judea.
  - East of the Jordan.
- The Questions.
  - Pharisees—Divorce?
  - Young Ruler—Eternal Life?
  - His Disciples—Who?
  - Peter—Rewards?
- The Answer.
  - Rewards.
  - A warning.
    - The first will be last.
    - The last will be first.
  - A parable.

"God is debtor to no man."

Jews vs. Gentiles

Prodigal son vs. brother.

many are called — few are chosen.

"Some people believe [the parable] is designed to teach that everyone will receive the same share in the eternal kingdom. This is not only irrelevant to the logic of the parable; it is *not true*. Neither is the purpose of the parable to proclaim the great evangelistic truth that salvation is by grace and not by works. … The great outstanding truth that is set forth is this: the divine Lord, whom everyone serves, estimates the value of the work we perform."

- Three Parables.
  - The Parable of the Money. Luke 19:12-28
  - The Parable of the Talents. Matthew 25:14-30
  - The Parable of the Laborers. Matthew 20:1-20

- Three Considerations.
  - The quantity of work.
  - The ability of the worker.
  - The motive of the worker.

The Parable of the Money. Luke 19:12-28

- The Charge.
  - Ten slaves (servants).
  - One mina each (~$2500).
    - Mina equals 50 shekels.
    - Shekel equals day's wage (~$50).
  - Do business.
- The Result.
  - The first slave. One mina → ten.
  - The second slave. One mina → five.
  - The third slave. One mina → no return.
- The Reward.
  - The first slave.
    - Ten cities.
    - Praise: "Well done, good slave."
  - The second slave.
    - Five cities.
    - Praise: None.
  - The third slave.
    - Principle taken away.
    - Condemnation: "You worthless slave."

The Parable of the Talents. Matthew 25:14-30

- The Charge.
  - Three slaves (servants).
  - According to ability.
    - To one, five talents (300 shekels).
    - To one, two talents.
    - To one, one talent.
  - Do business.

- The Result.
  - The first slave. Five talents → five.
  - The second slave. Two talents → two.
  - The third slave. One talent → no return.
- The Reward.
  - The first slave.
    - Put in charge of many things.
    - Praise: "Well done, good and faithful slave."
  - The second slave.
    - Put in charge of many things.
    - Praise: "Well done, good and faithful slave."
  - The third slave.
    - Principle taken away.
    - Condemnation: "You wicked and lazy slave."

The Parable of Laborers. Matthew 20:1-16

- The Charge.
  - At dawn. "A day's wage."
  - At nine. "Whatever is right."
  - At noon and three. "The same."
  - At five. "Go and join the other workers."
- The Reward.
  - The dawn patrol: a denarius
  - The late comers: a denarius
  - The 11th hour crew: a denarius

"This parable … teaches that a small quantity of work done with the right motive has a greater value than a large amount of work that is done with the wrong motive."

The Sin of Self-Righteousness

- Two Classes of Servants.
  - The First (shrewd and proud).
    - Jacob.
    - Simon. Matthew 26:6

- The elder brother. Luke 15:25
  - The Last (humble, generous, trusting).
    - Abraham.
    - The woman. Matthew 26:6
    - The prodigal brother. Luke 15:12
- Two Classes of Treatment.
  - The First.
    - Will be last.
    - Treated as slaves.
  - The Last.
    - Will be first.
    - Treated as sons.
- Three Cases of Self-Righteousness.
  - Those who practice self-denial on rare occasions.
  - Those whose sacrifice is more highly esteemed.
  - Those who reduce sacrifice to a system.

"All other things being equal, the sooner a person begins, the longer and the more earnestly a person is able to serve God; the harder he works, the better for him in the hereafter. If those who begin late in the day are graciously treated, it is in spite of their tardiness, not because of it. The fact that they have been idle so long is not to be commended—it is a sin. ... If it is wrong for those who greatly served the Lord to glory in their wonderful service, it is surely still more out of line—it is ridiculous—for anyone to take pride in the smallness of his. If the first does not have reason for boasting and self-righteousness, the last has even less."

Questions

1. Up to this point in your life, what are some of the sacrifices you have made for the sake of the kingdom of Christ?
2. As you studied this lesson, did the Lord speak to you of any sacrifices He would have you make for His kingdom?
3. How can you ensure that when you sacrifice for Christ in some way, that your motives remain pure? What would help you?

4. How are you tempted to violate the moral law of God as it pertains to *work* and *wages*? Do you struggle with pride?
5. How can you personally grow spiritually so that sacrificing for Christ's sake becomes a habit?

THE TRAINING OF THE TWELVE
30. The Second Lesson on the Doctrine of the Cross

Scripture

Matthew 20:17-28; Mark 10:32-45; Luke 18:31-34

Background

- The Setting.
    - Leaving Perea.
    - Toward Jerusalem.
- The Sequence.
    - The suffering of Jesus.
    - The request of the Two.
- The Request.
    - The requestor?
        - Salome (Zebedee).
        - James and John.
    - Preoccupation?
        - Thrones.
        - Kingdoms.

The Plot of James and John

- The Prelude.
    - Who is the greatest? Matthew 18:1
    - Whose throne is best?
- The Pattern.
    - Incident with the Samaritans. Luke 9:51-56
    - Incident regarding thrones.
- The Mother.
    - Bowing before the King.
    - "Grant me a simple request."
- Our Assessment.
    - The idea was not from God.
    - It is in line with human nature.

"We need to avoid two extremes: we should not be offended by their conduct, nor should we try to hide their true character in order to save their reputation."

- The Plot.

  So, what position would Peter have?

  - Irreverent and presumptuous.
    - Jesus would become their tool.
    - Jesus owed their mother.
  - Disrespectful and aggressive.
    - Characteristic of ambitious.
    - Insensitive to Jesus.
  - Ignorant and foolish.
    - Promotion in a secular state.
    - Promotion in the kingdom.
  - Selfish and inconsiderate.
    - Of their fellow disciples.
    - Of harmony within the body.

"'Grant us the places of honor and power, no matter what happens. We want these promotions even though everyone associated with us will become unhappy and disloyal, and what follows will be disorder, disaster, and chaotic confusion.' These consequences are certain to follow any promotion that is granted as a favor rather than by merit, both in the church and state."

Jesus' Response

- His Answer.
  - He overlooked their serious faults.
    - Presumption and selfishness.
    - Aggressiveness and pride.
  - He addressed their minor fault—ignorance.

- The Reply.
  - "You don't know what you are asking."
  - "Are you able to drink the cup ..."

"The way to thrones was the *via dolorosa* ("the way of sadness") of the cross. The palm-bearers in the realms of glory

91

would be those who had passed through great tribulation. The princes of the kingdom would be those who had drunk most deeply from His cup of sorrow."

- Their Reply.
  - Present: "We are able."
    - Quick.
    - Determined.
  - Future: Martyrdom.
    - James. Acts 12:2.
    - John. Revelation 1:9
- His Instruction.
  - His prerogative is not to grant position from partiality and favor.
  - His prerogative is to assign rightful places in the kingdom.
  - There is a natural relationship between:
    - The cup and the throne.
    - The suffering and the glory.

Suffering and Glory

"There is no better argument to support the doctrine of election than the simple truth that affliction is the education for heaven."

To understand + accept how the universe works?

Humility

"Pride and selfishness may provoke and grieve those who are humble and selfless, but they cause resentment to arise only in those who are proud and selfish."

Two Kingdoms

- Secular Kingdoms.
  - Rulers rule by birthright.
  - Rulers are served.
- The Divine Kingdom.
  - Rulers rule by faithfulness.

- Rulers serve.

"The true interests of an earthly kingdom would be promoted if it were governed as closely as possible with the laws of the kingdom—laws which cannot be changed."

What Did He Mean?

- There is a connection between self-sacrifice and leadership.
- There is an answer for self-indulgence and self-worship.

"Why should the son of a carpenter say about Himself, 'I did not come to be served?' The position and occupation of a servant was to be expected for someone of that background. The statement before us is rational and humble. It comes from one who, being in the form of God, freely assumed the form of a servant, and became obedient unto death for our salvation."

Questions

1. How much do you struggle with personal ambition (in business, in the church, etc.)?
2. What would you say are some of the characteristics of an ambitious spirit?
3. What instructions did Jesus give James and John that are helpful in understanding pride and ambition?
4. Are you willing to participate in the suffering of Christ, to drink of His cup, for the sake of the kingdom?
5. If we really knew what the answers to some of our prayers involved, we would not ask them. Do you ever pray for things for which you have not really thought through the possible outcomes?
6. What choices do you need to make, what habits do you need to establish, in order to become more of a servant-leader?

THE TRAINING OF THE TWELVE
31. The Doctrine of the Cross:
The Anointing in Bethany

Scripture

Matthew 26:6-13; Mark 14:3-9; John 12:1-8

Background

- The Setting.
  - Dinner in Bethany.
  - Simon the Leper.
  - Mary, Martha, Lazarus.
    - Dinner. Luke 10
    - Death. John 11
- The Sequence.
  - The plotting of the priests.
  - The anointing by Mary.
  - The treachery of Judas
- The Gift.
  - An alabaster vial.
    - Gypsum.
    - Box/flask.
  - Perfume of pure nard.
    - Asian herb.
    - Indian import.
  - The cost.
    - 300 denarii.
    - 1 year's wage.
- The Reaction.
  - Judas.
  - The Twelve.
  - Jesus.
"Was her action so supremely deserving of being associated with the Gospel throughout all time?"

Mary's Act

- Not about death.
- A festive honor.

The Alabaster Box as a Symbol

- Christ's Love for Us.
- Our Love for Christ.

"The anointing in Bethany has helped to preserve (to embalm, so to speak), the true meaning of the Savior's death. It has given us a symbolic act by which to understand His death. It has distributed around the cross an imperishable fragrance of self-forgetting love. It has decked the Savior's grave with flowers that will never wither. These flowers are raised for Jesus as well as for Mary and are a memorial stone that will endure throughout all generations."

Three Ways Their Works Resemble One Another

- Their Motive.
    - Mary loved Jesus wholeheartedly.
    - Jesus loves sinners wholeheartedly.
  "In the midst of all your speculations and theories on the grand theme of redemption, pay attention so that you do not fail to see in My death My loving heart, and the loving heart of My Father, revealed."
- Self-Sacrifice.
    - Mary spent all her resources.
    - He endured everything for us.
        - Humiliation, temptation.
        - Sorrow, suffering.
  "It was His pleasure to suffer for our redemption."
- Magnificence.
    - Mary's act appeared wasteful and extravagant.
    - Jesus shed His blood without measure.

"Magnificence which is misnamed *extravagance* and *waste* by those who do not know any better, is an invariable characteristic of all true love."

Three Aspects of Mary's Character

"Mary herself, in some important respects, is worthy to be lifted up as a model Christian."

- Her enthusiastic attachment to Christ.
  - Totally unselfish.
  - Unconcerned about consequences.
- There was freedom in her spirit.
  - She was creative.
  - She was original.
- There was nobility of spirit.
  - Usefulness vs. beautiful.
  - Chivalrous vs. commercial.

"The genius of Christianity is certainly not utilitarian. Its counsel is: 'Whatever is true, whatever is honorable, whatever is right, whatever is pure, whatever is lovely, whatever is of good repute, if there is any excellence and anything worthy of praise, let your mind dwell on these things.'(Philippians 4:8)"

Four Concluding Observations

- Mary was an example of genuine Christian piety.
- Being criticized is not proof of being wrong.
- If we can't be like Mary, at least we shouldn't be like Judas.
- Jesus' defense of Mary anticipated a worldwide Gospel.

Questions

1. Jesus wants us to surrender our lives to Him because we simply love Him so much. Do you, in fact, really love the Lord Jesus?

2. The reason Jesus endured the sorrow and suffering of the cross is because He loved sinners. Some Christians have a hard time believing that Jesus really loves them. What about you; do you know that Jesus loves you?
3. Mary's alabaster box. The widow's mite. Both were praised by Jesus. Both involved personal sacrifice. Have you come to the place in your relationship with Christ that you would readily make any sacrifice He asked you to make for His Kingdom and His honor?
4. In this regard, does your heart rule your head or your head rule your heart?
5. Explain why action is greater than scholarship.
6. Dr. Bruce says that "the power to do noble actions comes from love." How can your capacity to love Jesus grow so that you may serve Him better?
7. Do you have the freedom in your spirit to act like Mary? If not, what binds you? What stifles you?

THE TRAINING OF THE TWELVE
32. First Fruits of the Gentiles

Scripture

John 12:20-33

Background

- The Setting.
  - Passover in Jerusalem.
  - Mary's anointing.
  - Entering Jerusalem. John 12:12-19
    - On a colt.
    - Before the crowds.
- Samaritans and Greeks. John 4, John 12
  - Similarities.
    - Involve non-Jews
    - Jesus speaks of the future.
    - Jesus speaks of His Father's will.
  - Difference.
    - Samaria: enthusiasm, joy, hope.
    - Jerusalem: deep sadness.
- Jesus' Vision.
  - In Samaria.
    - Fields ready to harvest.
    - Reapers and sowers.
  - In Jerusalem.
    - World ready to harvest.
    - The seed that dies.

About the Greek Men

- What We Know.
  - They were Greeks.
  - They came to worship.

- What We Infer.
  - They were probably proselytes.
  - They knew about Jesus.
  - They were sincere inquirers.
    - Conclusion of Pharisees.
    - Reaction of Jesus.

Philip And Andrew

- Philip.
  - Brought Nathanael to Jesus.
  - Brought the Greeks to Jesus.

"It is one thing to introduce a devout Jew like Nathanael to Jesus. It is quite another thing to introduce Gentiles, no matter how devout they are. Philip is pleased that they are inquiring about his Master, but he is not sure how appropriate it would be to act on his first impulse."
- Andrew.
  - Preceded Philip in the faith.
  - Possibly Philip's mentor.

Jesus' Response to the Seekers

- His Heart Was Wounded.
  - The Pharisees
  - The Sadducees.
  - Ignorant crowds.
  - Indifferent followers.
  - Treacherous disciples.

"Rejected by His own people, He is consoled by the inspiring assurance that He will be believed on in the world. He will be accepted by all the nations for all of their salvation and all of their desire."

- His Heart Was Touched.
  - The people of Sychar. John 4
  - The Roman centurion. Matthew 8:5-13

99

- The woman of Tyre. Matthew 15:21-28
- The Samaritan leper. Luke 17:11-19
- The Greek seekers.

"This occurred when He thought about the unbelief and spiritual deadness of the chosen people for whom He had done so much. ... What sight is more moving than that of a human being seeking after God who is the fountain of light and life! ... But here we have the rare occurrence of men coming who have not been called. They were not sought by Christ."

Death and Fruitfulness

- A grain of wheat.
  - Dies when planted.
  - Bears much fruit.
- A person's life.
  - If sought—is lost.
  - If given—is gained.

"He is no fool who gives up that which he cannot keep to gain that which he cannot lose." Jim Elliott

An Application

- Fellowship between Himself and His followers.
  - With respect to death.
  - With respect to fruitfulness.
- Connection between suffering and glory.
  - With respect to honor.
  - With respect to power.

"This is the principle He teaches: in proportion to the depths that a man partakes in Christ's suffering in His state of humiliation, he will be a partaker of the glory, honor, and power which belongs to His state of exaltation. ... Bearing the cross—experiencing death—is the condition of fruit-bearing, both in the sense of personal sanctification and in the sense of effective service in the kingdom of God."

Questions

1. Jesus said that doing the Father's will is more important than life. How important is it for you to do your heavenly Father's will? Would you give up food for it (fasting)? Would you die for His glory (martyrdom)?
2. Why does one have to die in order to bear fruit?
3. What are some crosses God's children have to bear in order that they might bear more fruit?
4. What crosses are you currently bearing for His name's sake?
5. Will you surrender your life to Him each day, thanking Him for *everything* that comes into your life and refusing to become bitter or resentful for any suffering you endure?

THE TRAINING OF THE TWELVE
33. Discourse on the Last Things

Scripture

Matthew 21-25; Mark 11-13; Luke 19:29-48;20-21

Background

- The Setting.
  - Passover in Jerusalem.
  - Commuting from Bethany.
  - Panorama of the City.
- The Dialog.
  - Dilemma: By Whose Authority? Matthew 21:23-27.
  - Parable: Parable of the Two Sons. Matthew 21:28-32.
  - Parable: Parable of the Wicked Tenants. Matthew 21:33-46.
  - Parable: Parable of the Wedding Feast. Matthew 22:2-14.
  - Dilemma: Render to Caesar? Matthew 22:15-22.
  - Dilemma: Whose Wife is She? Matthew 22:23-33.
  - Dilemma: The Greatest Commandment? Matthew 22:33-40.
  - Dilemma: Whose Son is the Christ? Matthew 22:41-44.

In Defense of Jesus.

- We are awed.
- We are not surprised.

The Purpose of Jesus' Discourse

- The Main Point.
  - To expose the blind guides, **or**
  - To spare the people from delusion.
- The Main Audience.
  - The leaders, **or**

- The people.

"He told them [the people] that what He objected to was not so much the teaching of their guides, as their lives. They could follow all their precepts with little risk. But it would be fatal to follow their example."

The End of Jerusalem, the End of the World

"When they arrived at the Mount of Olives, the disciples sat down to take a leisurely view of the majestic buildings they had been talking about. ... The disciples are elated with pride as they gaze on the national structure. It is the glory of their country." (Mark 13:1)
- A Warning. Jesus (Mark 13:2)
    - Every building.
    - Total destruction.
- Two Questions. Peter, James, John, Andrew (Mark 13:3)
    - When will these things happen?
    - What will be the signs?

"The men thought that the two events referred to in the questions—the end of Jerusalem and the end of the world—would happen at the same time."

Six Precursors to the End of the World. Matthew 24:4-14

- The appearance of false Christs.
- Wars and rumors of wars.
- Famines, earthquakes, diseases.
- Persecution of believers.
- False prophets.
- Worldwide evangelization.

The End of Jerusalem. Matthew 24:15-28

- The Abomination.

103

- Destruction by Rome.
- Dispersion into the World.
- The Process.
  - Violence.
  - Apostasy and deception.

The Parable of the Fig Tree. Luke 21:29-32

- The Relevant Comparisons.
  - First buds = early summer.
  - Harvest = last judgment.
- The Relevant Parallels.
  - The fig tree = The Jewish nation.
  - The current generation = the beginning of Christendom.

"Christ did not mean that the generation that was living then was to witness the end, but in that generation all the things that form the incipient stage in the development would appear. It was the age of beginnings—shoots and blossoms, not fruit and harvest."

- Two Lessons.
  - For the Twelve—no restoration of the kingdom to Israel.
  - For all believers—take heed, keep on the alert.

The Parable of the Ten Virgins (Matthew 25:1-13)

"'Watching' does not imply sleepless worry and constant thought about the future. Rather, it suggests quiet, steady attention to present duties."

Questions

1. Here's a situation: You begin to notice that your pastor or priest seems to be getting ambitious and you are genuinely concerned. You are concerned about him personally and what could happen in your church as a result. What should you do?
2. Is it ever appropriate for you to rebuke another person or group of people as Jesus did the Pharisees? If so, what kind of situations do you think would allow for reproof? And what

concerns do you need to have about yourself as you move into these types of situations?

3. Jesus abhorred the hypocrisy of the Pharisees. Is it ever alright for us to abhor anything? If so, what?

4. The disciples could only see with the physical eye while Jesus saw "with the inward eye of prophecy." How can our eyes be opened to see as Jesus sees and to think as Jesus thought?

5. How can you take a greater part in seeking to evangelize the world?

6. Until the end of the world comes we are commanded to "be watchful." How can you be more alert during the time you have?

7. Are you currently being faithful to God in all that He has given you to do? If not, are you willing to repent and turn back to Him with all your heart?

8. Watch out for a negligent spirit!!! Why?

9. You will definitely be judged by the Great Judge (the Lord Jesus Christ) on the last day. Are you ready? If not, what do you need to change?

THE TRAINING OF THE TWELVE
34. Another Lesson in Humility: The Washing

Scripture

John 13:1-11

Background

- The Setting.
  - The last third of John's gospel.
  - The last week of Jesus' life.
  - The last hours with Jesus' disciples (Chapters 13-17, 20,21).
  - The feast of the Passover.
- The Last Supper.
  - His person.
    - All things had been given into His hands.
    - He had come forth from the Father.
    - And He was going back to God.
  - His disciples.
    - He had compassion for them.
    - He knew they would desert Him.
    - He humbled Himself for them all.

The Washing

- It was necessary.
  - Jesus had to humble Himself.
  - They would not humble themselves.
- They were proud.
  - Places at the table.
  - Places in the kingdom. Luke 22:16,16

"The method Jesus used to divert the minds of His disciples from unedifying topics, and to remove ambitious passions from their hearts, was a very effective one. Even His preliminary actions at the beginning of the feet-washing must have gone a long way to change their ruffled emotions. How the spectators must have stared and wondered as the Master rose from His seat, laid aside His outer cloak, gird Himself with a towel, and poured out water into a basin. He did all of this with self-control, composure, and deliberation!"

Peter's Reaction

- "Lord, do You wash my feet?"
  - It would damage the dignity of Jesus.
  - It outraged Peter's sense of reverence.
- "You do not realize [understand]."
  - I acknowledge this is offensive.
  - But permit me to do this.
  - You will understand later.

"Peter's first comment was the expression of sincere reverence. His second is simply the language of unmitigated irreverence and downright disobedience."

- "Never shall You wash my feet!"
  - He contradicts his Master.
  - He contradicts himself.
    - Self humiliation and self will.
    - Humility and pride.
    - Respect and disrespect.
- "You have no part with Me."
  "You have taken a very serious position, Simon Peter. The question at hand is simply this: 'Are you, or are you not, to be admitted into My kingdom—to be a true disciple, and to have a true disciple's reward.'"
  Peter's attitude was:
  - He would not allow any behavior that seemed inconsistent with the personal dignity of Jesus.
  - He would adopt as his rule of conduct his own judgment, and he would prefer that over Christ's will.

"The first principle sweeps away Christ's whole condition and experience of *humiliation*. The last one erodes the foundation of Christ's *lordship*."

"In short, the incarnation, atonement, and Christ's whole earthly experience of temptation, hardship, indignity, and sorrow, must go if Jesus is not allowed to wash a disciple's feet. It is also clear that Christ's lordship comes to a complete stop if a disciple can give Him orders and say, 'You will never wash my feet.'"

If Christ Is Not Able To Humble Himself

- He can have no part with us.
- We can have no part with Him.
    - We cannot share His fellowship with the Father.
    - We cannot receive His brotherly acts of kindness.
    - He cannot deliver us from the curse of the law.
    - He cannot deliver us from the fear of death.
    - He cannot help us when we are tempted.
    - He cannot wash our souls.

"Is there room for love in a Being who cannot humble Himself to be a servant?"

Jesus' Last Word on the Matter

- Physical Cleansing.
    - A bath gets the big stuff.
    - Sponging gets the travel grime.
- Spiritual Cleansing.
    - Salvation gets the big stuff—our sin (sin nature).
    - Confession gets the travel grime—our sins (trespasses).

Questions

1. We read how Jesus' washing of the disciple's feet affected them. How does this account of His startling humility affect you?

2. Like Peter, we are capable of expressing the "language of unmitigated irreverence and downright disobedience, by resisting Christ when He has made His will known." What are some ways we are guilty of doing this?
3. How can we be guilty of giving orders to Christ, rather than submitting ourselves completely to His will?
4. Do we have to understand—through our reason or the perception of goodness—the Lord's will before we obey? Illustrate.
5. Would you say you are seeking to obey the Lord in all areas of your life? Are there any areas you need to surrender to His lordship? If so, would you do so now?

THE TRAINING OF THE TWELVE
35. Another Lesson In Humility: The Explanation

Scripture

John 13:12-20

Background

- The Setting.
  - The last third of John's gospel.
  - The last week of Jesus' life.
  - The last hours with Jesus' disciples. (Chapters 13-17, 20, 21)
  - The Feast of the Passover.
- The Washing.
  - The need of the disciples.
    - Meekness.
    - Brotherly kindness.
    - Humility.
  - The example of the Master.
    - He becomes the servant of the household.
    - He performs the menial duties of a servant.
    - He humbled Himself for them all.
  - The humility of the Master.
    - Is not misinformed.
    - Is that of a king—a Divine Being.
  - The expectation of Jesus.
    - As their Teacher, it is their business to learn His doctrine.
    - As their Master, it is their duty to obey Him.

The Rarity and Difficulty of Humility

- Humility is Rare.
  - It is lofty and noble.
  - It is contrary to the human heart.

- It is foreign to today's culture.

"Are people generally content to be in the humblest place and to seek the happiness of others by serving them?"

- The Spirit within Us.
  - Envious. Desiring what others have or are.
  - Ambitious. Striving for positions of influence.
  - Mistaken. Thinking happiness is to be served.
  - Inflated. Seeking exemption from servant tasks.
- Humility is Difficult.

"No proof is needed to convince the sincere disciple of Jesus that the task given him by his Lord is difficult. He knows from experience how far his conduct lags behind his knowledge. He knows how hard it is to move from admiring a goodness that is not of this world to imitating it in practice."

- How We Cope.
  - We exaggerate its difficulty.
  - We say it is utopian and impracticable.
  - We say it is a beautiful, unattainable ideal.

"When he [the sincere disciple of Jesus] has to close his New Testament and go away into the rude, ungodly, matter-of-fact world, and be a Christ-like person there, and do the things that he knows so well (he even considers himself blessed because he knows them), behold what a descent!"

A Three-Fold Blessedness

"The happiness of those who are enabled to practice this virtue is in direct proportion to its difficulty and rarity. They have a three-fold blessedness."

- Joy.
  - Of doing a difficult task.
  - Of having the mind of the meek and humble One.
- Approval.
  - A teacher is pleased with understanding.
  - A master is pleased with obedience.

111

"It is often true that we will please other people the least when we are pleasing the Lord the most. ... But if Christ approves of us, we may very well have to do without the sympathy and approval of other people. Their approval is, at best, a comfort. His is a matter of life and death."

- Escape from Guilt.
  - All believers know the standard.
  - Few believers actually fulfill it.

One Who Knows, But Will Not Do

- Judas, and Others.
  - Put sentiment in the place of action.
  - Put admiration in the place of imitation.
  - Promise is offered in the place of performance.
  - Speaking the right words is substituted for doing the right deeds.

  "Jesus could put up with the weakness of sincere disciples. But not with the Judas character."
- The Eleven, and Others.
  - Tried to fulfill their Master's will.
  - Served one another in love.

Questions

1. Jesus became a model of humility for all Christians and He demands that we pay attention to His behavior and that we emulate it. Will you make this effort and ask the Lord to enable you to follow Him in the power of His Spirit?
2. What excuses do we tend to make for not being humble?
3. How does your involvement in and with the world hinder you from becoming the humble person the Lord wants you to be?
4. What are some practical ways we can demonstrate humility? In the home? In the neighborhood? At work? At church?

THE TRAINING OF THE TWELVE
36. In Memoriam: Fourth Lesson on the Doctrine of the Cross

Scripture

Matthew 26:26-29; Mark 14:22-25; Luke 22:17-20

Background

- The Setting.
    - The last hours with Jesus' disciples.
    - The Feast of the Passover.
    - The Last Supper.
- The Lord's Death.
    - What it wasn't.
        - A calamity or dark disaster.
        - A fatal blow for the cause.
        - An evil that was to be overruled.
    - What it was.
        - An event that fulfilled His purpose.
        - It would provide blessings to the world.
        - It was His own voluntary act.
        - It initiated a new covenant.
        - It sealed a new testament.
        - It fulfilled the Mosaic rituals.

"We are used to explaining the Supper by His death, rather than the death by the Supper. It may be profitable here to reverse the process."

In Memory of His Death

- The Lord's Supper Refers to His Death.
    - It is not in memory of Him in general.
    - It is not in memory of His excellent life.

113

- His Death Was of Utmost Importance.
  - Because of its tragic character?
  - Because it excites our feelings?
  - Because it elicits our sympathy?
  - Because of the awful wrong?
  - Because it marked the world with infamy?
  - Because it was glorious?
  - Because He would be a martyr?

The Benefits of His Death

- His Blood.
  - Shed for the forgiveness of sins.
    "The sin-offering of blood will be converted into a thank-offering of wine, a cup of salvation to be drunk with grateful, joyful hearts by all who through faith in His sacrifice have received the pardon for their sins."
  - Signified a new testament.
    "The new covenant concerns the many, not the few—not Israel alone, but all nations. It is a Gospel which He offers to all sinners. The cup is the seal of this new covenant."
- His Body.
  - Is the bread of God for our souls.
  - Is our spiritual nourishment.
    "Christ is the Bread of Life in all of His offices. As a *Prophet*, He supplies the bread of divine truth to feed our minds. As a *Priest*, He furnishes the bread of righteousness to satisfy our troubled consciences. As a *King*, He presents Himself to us as an object of devotion that will fill our hearts, and whom we may worship without fear of idolatry."

"The Lord's Supper commemorates the Lord's death. ... And He meant for it to be repeated, not only by the Apostles, but by all Christians in all ages until He comes again."

How to Observe the Supper

- In a spirit of humility.
- With confession and thanksgiving to God for:
    - His covenant of grace.
    - His mercy in Christ.
- With love for Him who:
    - Washes away sins.
    - Nourishes the soul.
- Giving Him all glory and dominion.
- With love for all true believers as brothers.

Questions

1. Jesus relied on the Father's promise and endured the cross because of the "joy set before Him" (Hebrews 12:2). We are to practice the same principle. We are to be faithful and not live for ourselves, but for others, for the church, for the whole world. In what ways do you make sacrifices for the cause of Christ and His kingdom?
2. Reflect on the following benefits of the death of Christ.
    - Our sins are pardoned. Have you been forgiven and cleansed by the blood of Christ? Do you have assurance of salvation through His atoning work?
    - Our minds are fed with the bread of Divine truth. Do you consistently and faithfully spend time reading, studying, and meditating on God's Word.
    - Our troubled consciences are satisfied by the bread of righteousness. Are you confessing sins and receiving His forgiveness and freedom from guilt?
    - Our Hearts are filled with Christ and we respond in worship. Are you allowing anyone or anything to replace your single-minded devotion to Christ?
    - We are helped to appropriate Christ as our spiritual food more and more abundantly. Are you growing spiritually?
    - Our faith is strengthened. Is this true of you?

- We are reminded to pray for an increasing number of people to experience salvation. Are you praying for people to come to Christ? Are you asking God to give you opportunities to share the gospel with others?
3. How will today's lesson change the way you celebrate the Lord's Supper?

THE TRAINING OF THE TWELVE
37. Judas Iscariot

Scripture

Matthew 26:20-23; Mark 14:17-21; Luke 22:21-23; John 13:21-30

Background

- The Setting.
  - The last hours with Jesus' disciples.
  - The Feast of the Passover.
  - The Last Supper.
  - The Lord's Supper.
- The Man.
  - His Background. Joshua 15:25
    - Kerioth.
    - Judean.
  - His Biography.
    - His call. Matthew 10:4; Mark 3:19; Luke 6:16
    - His office. John 13:29
    - His preoccupation. John 12:1-8; Matthew 26:6-13; Mark 14:3-9
    - His arrangement. Matthew 26:14-16; Mark 14:10-11; Luke 22: 3-6
    - His treachery. Matthew 26:47-49; Mark 14:43-45; Luke 22:47-48; John 18:1-5
    - His end. Matthew 27:3-5; John 17:12; Acts 1:16-25
  - His Evaluation.
    - In Galilee. John 6:70-71
    - At the Washing. John 13:26-30
    - At the Supper. John 17:12

Why Did Jesus Choose Judas?

"One has to wonder how such a man ever got in. ... These two points are certain: 1) on the one hand, Judas did not become a follower of Jesus with treacherous intentions; and 2) Jesus did not choose Judas to be one of the Twelve because He foreknew that he would eventually become a traitor."

- Judas was eligible.
  - He must have had qualities.
    - Zeal?
    - Apparent godliness?
    - Behavior?
  - He may have been like Eliab. 1 Samuel 16:6
- Judas was flawed.
  - He knew what was good and approved it.
  - He did not consciously practice it.
  - He leaned in his feelings, imagination and intellect toward things noble and holy.
  - He was a slave of worthless, selfish passions in his will and conduct.

"He would always put himself first, yet he could zealously devote himself to doing good deeds when his personal interests were not compromised. ... Anyone who loves himself more than any other person, no matter how good, or any cause, no matter how holy, is always capable of bad faith. He is a traitor in the heart from the beginning."

Why Did Judas Turn Traitor?

- The Surface Explanation.
  - He was greedy and covetous.
  - He was corrupt.
  - His primary passion was financial.

"It is extremely rare for a man who is filled with greed to feel remorse over the crimes he committed because of greed. It is the nature of greed to destroy the conscience and to make all things, no matter how sacred, corrupt."

- The Deeper Explanation.
  - He was not a Galilean.
    - He was an outsider.
    - His deeds were noticed.

118

- Jesus saw through him.
  - Jesus probably tried to change him.
  - Love turned to hatred.
- He was opportunistic.
  - He saw impending catastrophe.
  - He saw coming opportunity.

"These observations help bring the crime of Judas Iscariot within the range of human experience. ... For it is not in our best interest to think of the traitor as an absolutely unique character, as the solitary, perfect incarnation of satanic wickedness. It would be better for us to think of his crime in a way that our minds make us ask, like the disciples, 'Is it I?'"

Questions

1. The outward appearance of Judas did not match his heart. Are you, in any way, living the life of a hypocrite (a play-actor or pretender)?
2. We can fool other people, but we cannot escape the all-seeing and all-knowing eye of our God. Are there any secret sins that you are harboring in your heart or committing in your life? If so, would you be willing to confess them and repent of them now?
3. Are you confident, as you examine your life—your behavior, your words, your thoughts, your speech—that you are truly a child of God? Is the fruit there? Remember the *assurance of salvation* is based, not only on the promises of God (1 John 5:13) and the internal witness of the Holy Spirit (Romans 8:16), but also on a changed life (James 1:22).
4. Judas gave the devil an opportunity. And he took it. What are some ways we can give Satan opportunities in our lives? How can we close the door so he cannot use us for his purposes— purposes that are contrary to those of our Lord?
5. Have others ever treated you with hatred or misunderstanding? Is the Lord asking you to love someone whom you find difficult to love—perhaps someone you don't trust?

Remember Jesus who patiently endured Judas for 3 1/2 years. We must go to Him for the enabling to love others the way we cannot in our own strength.

THE TRAINING OF THE TWELVE
38. The Dying Parent and the Little Ones: Words of Comfort and Counsel to the Sorrowing Children

Scripture

John 13:31-35; 14:1-4,15-21

Background

- The Setting.
  - The last hours with His disciples.
  - The last hours of His life.
- The Master.
  - His Destiny. John 13:31-32
    - He would be glorified.
    - God would be glorified in Him.

  "But He also remembered that He had all around Him disciples to whom, in their weakness, His decease and departure would mean nothing less than bereavement and devastation. Therefore, He immediately turned His thoughts to them and began to say things that were appropriate to their inward condition and their outward situation."

  - His Demeanor. "My little children …"
  - His Dialog.
    - A dying parent addressing His children.
    - A dying Lord addressing His servants, friends, and representatives.

Jesus' First Dying Counsel

- His Counsel. "I am going away; in My absence find comfort in one another's love."

  "And when His followers expressed love to one another, and had the same spirit Jesus had, and were ready to do the same things He did, the world would stare—because it was new. They would be amazed and ask where it came from. The world would perceive that the men who loved in this way had been with Jesus."

- New Things.
  - A new covenant.
  - A new sacrament.
  - A new commandment.

"So He conferred on it [this new commandment] all of the dignity and importance of a new commandment, and made the love that was required in it to be the distinctive mark of Christian discipleship."

Jesus' Second Dying Counsel

- His Counsel. "I am going away; but it is to My Father's house and, in due time, I will come back and take you there."
- His Provision.
  - The Father's protection.
  - The Son's peace.

"In essence, He says to them, 'I am going to leave you, My children; but do not be afraid. You will not be like orphans in the world—defenseless and not provided for. God, My Father will take care of you. Trust in Divine Providence, and let peace rule in your hearts.'"

- Their Rewards.
  - The Father's house.
  - The Son's preparation.

Jesus' Third Dying Counsel

- His Counsel. "I am going away; but even when I am away, I will be with you in the person of My *alter ego*, the Comforter."
- The Comforter.
  - The consciousness of His own presence.
  - The manifestation of His spiritual return.

"The Spirit would make the absent Jesus present to them again by bringing to their remembrance all His words, by bearing witness of Him, and by guiding them into an intelligent apprehension of all Christian truth."

- The Introduction.
  - "If you love Me."
  - Do not sorrow.

"In His first great sermon (the Sermon on the Mount) Jesus had said, 'Blessed are the pure in heart for they shall see God' (Matthew 5:8). In His farewell address to His disciples, He says in essence: 'Be pure in heart, and through the indwelling Spirit of Truth you will see Me, even when I have become invisible to the world.'"

Questions

1. Do you allow yourself to come into the presence of the Lord with your weaknesses, doubts, and questions? How do Jesus' words "little children," first spoken to the Apostles, have relevance to your life?
2. What would be the effect on the world if Christians loved one another as Christ loved them?
3. Do you believe that God your Father will take care of you throughout your life? Why or why not?
4. What are some of the rewards you can expect to receive in heaven because of the death and resurrection of Jesus Christ?
5. Do you understand the ministry of the Holy Spirit in the lives of believers?
6. Explain the phrase "Walking in the Spirit." How can you practice this discipline every moment?
7. Is there any commandment of God that you are violating in your life right now? Are you willing to confess it and forsake it (repent)?
8. What can you expect from God if you live a life of obedience to Him?

THE TRAINING OF THE TWELVE
39. The Dying Parent and the Little Ones:
The Children's Questions, and the Farewell

Scripture

John 13:36-38; 14:5-7,8-14,22-31

Background

- The Setting.
  - The last hours with His disciples.
  - The last hours of His life.
- The Master.
  - His Destiny. John 13:31-32
    - He would be glorified.
    - God would be glorified in Him.
  - His Demeanor. "My little children …"
  - His Dialog.
    - A dying parent addressing His children.
    - A dying Lord addressing His servants, friends, and representatives.

Peter's Questions

- The First Question. "Lord, where are You going?"
  "He was thinking, "Where You go, I will go.'"
- Jesus' Answer. "Where I go, you cannot follow; but you shall follow later."
  "With this answer, He demonstrated that He was dealing with children. He does not expect heroic behavior from Peter and his fellow disciples as the crisis approaches. He does expect that they will ultimately play the hero. They will follow Him on the martyr's path bearing the cross."
- The Second Question. "Lord, *why* can I not follow You right now?"
  - He probably was hurt by the low opinion of his courage.

- He impulsively assured Jesus of his confidence—and devotion.
- Jesus' Answer. "You will deny Me three times."
  - His first answer was indirect and evasive; this one too plain to be misunderstood.
  - Peter needed to be told once and for all who he was, by his Master.
  - He had been admonished on more than one occasion for his failures:
    - Being too pushy.
    - Over-confidence.
  - Specific correction had not produced deep impressions.

"There was an urgent need for him to be taught a lesson that he would never forget. It would be a word of correction that would be indelibly imprinted on the erring disciple's memory. …. Being converted from self-confidence and self-will to meekness and modesty, he will finally be prepared to strengthen others, to be a shepherd to the weak, and, if necessary, to bear his cross and follow his Master through death to glory"

Thomas' Question

- The Question. "How do we know the way?"
  - He doesn't, like Peter, ask where? He is too despondent to want to know too much.
  - His question is almost an apology. It is not a request for knowledge but an excuse for ignorance.
- Jesus' Answer. "I am the way, the truth, and the life; no one comes to the Father but through Me."
  - The Father not the Father's house.
  - Jesus Himself becomes the way.

"If you do not know anything about the place called heaven, at least know that you have a Father there. As for the way to heaven, let that be Me. If you know Me, you do not need any additional knowledge. If you believe in Me, you can look

125

forward to the future—even to death itself—without fear or concern."

Philip's Request

- The Question. "Lord, Show us the Father, and it is enough for us."
  - Philip could not agree with Jesus' statement, "You know Him [the Father]."
  - Seeking to know God the Father is man's highest aspiration.
  - Philip wanted to see God with his physical eyes as he saw Jesus.
- Jesus' Reply. "Have I been so long with you, and yet you have not come to know Me."
  - Their lack of spiritual capacity must have been disappointing.
    "They did not have a clear, full, consistent, spiritual conception of the mind, heart, and character of the man Christ Jesus, in whom all the fullness of deity dwelt (Colossians 1:19). They would not understand these concepts until the Spirit of Truth, the promised Comforter, came. The very thing He would do for them was to show them Christ."
  - To be ignorant of the Father was a denial of His divinity.
    "Now you know how to see Him. You do it by reflecting on your relationship with Me. The only reason for the statements made to Philip concerning the close relationship between the Father and the Son was to impress upon the disciples the great truth that the solution to all religious difficulties, and the fulfillment of all longings, was to be found in knowing Christ."

Judas' [Not Iscariot] Question

- The Question. "You are going to disclose Yourself to us and not to the world?"

126

- How is this possible?
- Why would You do this?

• Jesus' Answer. "If anyone loves Me, he will keep My word, and My Father will love him, and We will come to him, and make Our abode with him.

"The divine trinity—Father, Son, and Spirit—will truly dwell with the faithful disciple who is very concerned about making every effort to keep My commandments."

The Farewell

"Peace I leave with you; My peace I give to you; not as the world gives, do I give to you."

Questions

1. Whether we like it or not, it is good for us when the Lord deals bluntly with us and lets us know what He thinks about us. Think back over your spiritual journey and recall a time when the Lord got your attention and dealt with something in your life. How did you change?
2. What can you know about God from creation? List 3 or 4 specific things that you have personally observed.
3. As you know, it is not enough to *know about* God. We must *know* Him. What do you need to do to make knowing Him your highest priority?
4. Is it possible to see Jesus without really seeing Him? Is it possible to know Him without really knowing Him? Explain the difference between seeing Him with physical eyes and seeing Him with the eyes of the spirit.
5. Jesus always referred to God as *Father*. Individuals refer to God as the Deity; the Almighty; the Infinite, Eternal Abstraction; the Judge; the Lawgiver; the Absolute. Why is the term *Father* so important to believers?
6. How can you experience peace of heart and mind?

THE TRAINING OF THE TWELVE
Dying Charge to the Future Apostles
40. The Vine and Its Branches

Scripture

John 15:1-15

Background

- The Setting.
    - The Last Supper.
    - The final charge.
- The Message.
    - You did not choose Me.
    - I chose and appointed you.
    - You should go and bear fruit.
    - Your fruit should remain.
- The Symbol.
    - Why He chose it.
    - What it communicates.

Personal Holiness and Fruit-bearing

- What Kind of Fruit?
    - Omitted?
    - Apostles?
    "The fruit He is looking for is the spread of the Gospel and bringing souls into the kingdom of God."
- What about Personal Holiness?
    - It is not the fruit itself.
    - It is the means of production.
- What About Unproductive Branches?
    - Some are cut off—unbelievers.
    - Some are pruned—believers.

The Conditions for Fruitfulness

"Abide in Me, and I in you."

- The Branch Abides in the Vine *Structurally*.
  - Holding on to His teachings and doctrine.
  - Professing His truth; being His witnesses.
- The Vine Abides in the Branch *Vitally*.
  - The indwelling Spirit.
  - The Spirit of truth.

Both types of abiding are necessary! "On the one hand, a person may strictly embrace Christian orthodoxy, but have little or no spiritual life. On the other hand, another person may have a certain amount of spiritual vitality, great morals, and in some respects, desires that are similar to a Christian, but has seriously departed from the faith. ... Dead orthodoxy is notoriously impotent. ... Heresies—not abiding in the teachings of Christ—are equally helpless."

- The Responsibility of Branches.
  - Overcoming the worries of life.
  - Guarding the insidious influence of wealth
  - Opposing the lusts of the flesh.
  - Checking the passions of the soul.

"He finally resolves the whole issue in plain language—they must keep His commandments. If they diligently and faithfully do their part, the divine Husbandman assures them that He will not fail to give them everything that is necessary for the most abundant fruitfulness."

Quantity and Quality

"Jesus made it clear to the disciples that He expected them to bear, not only fruit, but *much* fruit. This fruit would not just be abundant in *quantity*, but good in *quality*."

- First Motivation for Fruitfulness.
  - The Father is glorified.
  - Proof of discipleship.
- Second Motivation for Fruitfulness.
  - For His own joy in us.
  - For our joy to be full.
- Third Motivation for Fruitfulness.
  - We are his friends.
  - He has asked us.

Love One Another

"He evidently intends for the disciples to understand that abiding in each other by love is just as necessary to their success as their common abiding in Him by faith."

Questions

1. As a Christian, you "must take His place, act in His stead, and carry on the work He had begun." Remember the words, "My disciples—fruit, fruit?" In what ways are you currently bearing fruit?
2. Personal holiness is required as a means by which fruit is produced. Are you living in obedience to God's word and striving to please Christ (Ephesians 5:10)? If not, are you willing to honestly face your sin(s) and repent (to change your mind with a resulting change in behavior)?
3. What are some of the consequences you could face for *not* bearing fruit?
4. What specific things could you do so that you can more faithfully abide in Christ?
5. What are some of the ways the Father has pruned you in the past? What were the results in your life?
6. What impact did the chapter have on you?
7. Would you like to be more fruitful?
8. What do you sense you need to do to be a more fruitful Christian?

9. Would you begin praying today that the Lord would direct and empower you to bear much fruit?

THE TRAINING OF THE TWELVE
41. Dying Charge to the Future Apostles:
Tribulations and Encouragements

Scripture

John 15:18-27; 16:1-15

Background

- The Setting.
  - The Last Supper.
  - The final charge.
- The Message.
  - Master and slaves.
  - Coming persecution.
  - Coming Comforter.
  - Encouragement.

"All great people who are involved in God's work, and whose fruit has staying power, will certainly experience sorrow to a greater or lesser degree. One of the penalties of moral greatness and spiritual power is to be hated and treated in an evil manner. Or, to put it in a different way, it is one of the *privileges* Christ confers on His friends."

Resources for Facing Trouble

- Know What to Expect.
  - The world's hatred is certain.
  - His disciples will be outcasts.
  "They will make you outcasts from the synagogue, but an hour is coming for everyone who kills you to think that he is offering a service to God." John 16:2
- His Suffering was Worse.
  - The One who has been hated is the Lord.
  - The ones who will be hated are servants.

"The servants should be ashamed to complain about difficult circumstances when their Master was not exempt from them (nor did He wish to be).

- Suffering Goes with the Turf.
  - Either they forfeit the honor, privileges and hope of their position, or
  - Accept the hatred of those who love darkness above light.

Jesus Explains the World's Hatred

- Those Who Hate.
  - Guilty of unbelief.
  - Hate without cause.
  "They hated Someone whose whole character and conduct, works and words, should have won their faith and love."
- Who Has Not Hated?
  - With bad feelings.
  - With bitter words.
  "They hated genuine goodness and could not rest until they had thrown it out of the world and nailed it to a cross. With the history and sayings of Christ right in front of us, we must be careful not to be too sympathetic toward those who live in unbelief."

Hope for a Brighter Future

- A Changed Opinion.
  - The testimony of the Spirit.
  - The testimony of the Apostles.
  "He quickly suggested that the disciples as well as the Spirit of truth would have a part in the honorable work of redeeming their Master's name and character from disgrace."
- A Noble Cause.
  "He told them that they would suffer for a cause that was favored by Heaven and for honoring the One they loved more than life. ... Who would not be happy to be rebuked and treated badly for a Name that is worthy to be above every

name, especially if he was assured that the sufferings he endured directly contributed to the exaltation of that blessed Name to its proper place of sovereignty?
- For His sake we are killed.
- For His sake we are counted as sheep.

"But who cares? The church is spreading; believers are multiplying on every front. They are springing up a hundred-fold from the seed of the martyr's blood; the name of our Lord is being magnified. Therefore we will gladly suffer for bearing witness to the truth."

The Primary Source of Tribulations

- The World.
  - Non-religious, skeptical, easy going, gross living.
  - Those who do not claim to know God.
- The Enemy.
  - Those who regularly attended synagogue.
  - Those who claim to be the people of God.

"The same phenomenon has reappeared in the Christian Church. The world that is most opposed to Christ, Antichrist itself, is not to be found in the world of the unbelievers, but in the church; not among those who are non-religious and skeptical, but among those who claim to be God's people."

Jesus Helps the Apostles Cope

- He apologizes for speaking of painful matters.
- He rebukes them for their silence.

The Holy Spirit's Ministry

- He convicts the world concerning sin.
- He convicts the world concerning righteousness.
- He convicts the world concerning judgment.

"The idea is that the Spirit would use the exaltation of Christ to make people sincerely think about the whole subject of righteousness; to show them the absolute rotten character of their own righteousness, whose crowning accomplishment was to crucify Jesus; to bring home to their hearts the solemn truth that the Crucified One was the Just One."

Delayed Changes

"It was necessary for the personal ministry of Jesus to come to an end before the ministry of the Spirit began ... the Spirit does not speak on his own. He simply takes the things that relate to Christ and shows them to unbelievers so they can be brought to conviction and conversion. He shows them to believers so they can be enlightened and sanctified."

Questions

1. How do you handle rejection and hatred when you take a stand for Christ?
2. Re-examine the three resources Jesus provided for the Twelve to give them courage. Explain how these same resources can give you the courage you need to face the opposition from the world.
3. What are some of the indications that the world has entered the church, that is, that some of those who are most opposed to Christ are in the church? Has this happened in your church?
4. What is the role of the Holy Spirit in preparing you to reach the unbelievers you are seeking to reach with the Gospel?
5. What is the role of the Holy Spirit in preparing *unbelievers* to be receptive to the claims of Christ?
6. What is the role of the Holy Spirit in the life of *believers*?

THE TRAINING OF THE TWELVE
42. Dying Charge to the Future Apostles:
The Little While, and the End of the Discourse

Scripture

John 16:16-33

Background

- The Setting.
    - The Last Supper.
    - The final paradox.
- The Riddle.
    - A little while and you will not behold Me.
    - Again a little while and you will see Me.

"The riddle served at least one purpose—it brought the disciples out of the numbness of their grief and, for a brief moment, awakened their curiosity. ... It surprised them, but did not convey any meaning. Those who heard him were forced to confess, 'We don't know what He is talking about.'"

Sorrow Now, Joy Later

- Key to Understanding.
    - The first clause refers to the physical sense.
    - The second clause refers to the spiritual sense.
    "Immediately after that time [His ascension], they began to see Him in another way. A new understanding of His life sweetly crept into the eyes of their souls."
- An Important Comparison.
    - The crisis the disciples would experience.
    - The crisis of a mother giving birth.
- Several Interpretations.
    - Jesus is the mother, the sorrow is His death.

- The disciples are the mother, the sorrow is His death.
  - Joy comes after the resurrection.
  - Joy comes with the Holy Spirit.
  - Joy comes at His second coming.

Three Aspects of Spiritual Illumination

"He was alluding to their initiation into the highest level of the Christian mysteries when they would see things clearly that had been unintelligible before."

- A Greater Comprehension of Truth.
  - No more children's questions.
  - No more cloudy mirror. 1 Corinthians 13:12
  "The degree of illumination that the Apostles received might be described, without exaggerating, as that of men who did not need to ask questions any longer."
- Unlimited Influence with God through Prayer.
  - Power to perform miracles and heal diseases.
  - Power to prophesy—to foretell the future.
  - Power of providence—to work situations for the good of the cause.
  "The substance of the promise—though not its miraculous elements—was made to all who aspire to Christian maturity, and is fulfilled to all who reach it."
- An Enlarged Heart.
  - For desiring, asking and expecting great things.
    - No more petty desires.
    - Kingdom-sized requests.
  - To experience fullness of joy.
    - In His work in their hearts.
    - In His work in the world.
  "How many people have enlarged hearts with great visions? ... How many earnestly and passionately desire the conversion of those who are lost, long for the unity, peace, and purity of the church, and the growth of righteousness in society at large?"

Near the End of the Discourse

- Figurative Language.
  vs.
- Plain Talk.

"Shortly afterwards, the disciples would begin to experience the fulfillment of Philip's prayer, 'Lord, show us the Father, and it is enough for us.'"

God Hears Prayer

"My Father will not need to be begged to hear you, the men who have been with Me through all of My trials, who have loved Me with all of your hearts, who have believed that I am the Christ, the Son of the living God, while the world at large has regarded Me as an impostor and a blasphemer. Because of the things you have done for His Son, My Father loves you—in a sense, He considers Himself a debtor to you."

True Faith

"I came forth from the Father, and have come into the world; I am leaving the world again, and going to the Father."

- They believed the first clause. Childlike faith.
- They didn't understand the second. True faith.

"As a result of their ignorance, their faith would not carry them through the evil hour that was now very close. The death of their Master … would take them by surprise and make them flee like panic-stricken sheep attacked by wolves."

Jesus' Consolation as He Faces Death

- He had a good conscience.

- He had the approval of the Father.

Jesus Christ, Our Representative

"Jesus fought his battle, not as a private person, but as a public figure, as a representative for every person. And everyone is welcome to claim the benefits of his victory, such as the pardon of sin, the power to resist the evil one, and admission into the everlasting kingdom. ... we ought to look to him as our head in all things."

- As our King, we ought to lay down the weapons of our rebellion.
- As our Priest, we ought to receive from Him pardon for our sins.
- As our Lord, we ought to be ruled by His will, defended by His might, guided by His grace.

Questions

1. A.B. Bruce compares the growth of the disciples' faith to the developmental stages in the life of a butterfly—the transition from the chrysalis to the time when their wings are fully developed. He used the cocoon to represent their ignorant, implicit faith, and the fully developed butterfly to represent "a faith that was developed and intelligent." Take a few moments to quietly reflect on the nature of your own faith. At this time in your spiritual journey, how would you describe your faith (i.e., on the continuum between the cocoon and the butterfly, where would you place your faith)?
2. Think about the ministry of the Holy Spirit and the part He plays in bringing spiritual illumination to believers. In your relation to Him, how can you gain "a greater comprehension of truth"?
3. How can you have "unlimited influence with God in prayer"?
4. What steps do you need to take to ensure that your heart is becoming enlarged—that is, that you are learning to make

"large demands on the riches of God's grace for yourself, the Church, and the World"?

5. Do you regularly experience real joy? Think about this for a moment. How much are you tied to the world's view that one can only be truly happy when life's circumstances are favorable (and sad or depressed when things are going wrong)? Christ told us that we would have joy in Him. What does it mean to find our joy in Christ and how do you appropriate this extraordinary joy?

6. Do you have confidence that God hears your prayers? What questions or concerns do you have in this area?

7. When you experience difficult problems or challenges in life, why is it necessary and important to do so with a clear conscience and the Father's approval?

8. In what specific ways can you claim the benefits of the victory that Christ won in His battle over sin and death?

THE TRAINING OF THE TWELVE
43. The Intercessory Prayer

Scripture

John 17

Background

- The Setting.
  - The Last Supper.
  - The High Priestly Prayer.
- The Prayer.
  "Our determined purpose for years was to read it in solemn, reverent silence without comment. Reluctantly, we now depart from that position. We feel compelled for three reasons."
  - Jesus prayed audibly for the instruction of the eleven.
  - John recorded it for the benefit of the church.
  - God preserved it for our understanding.

Jesus Prays for Himself

"The prayer Jesus prayed for Himself contains just one petition with two reasons added."
- The Petition: "Glorify Thy Son."
  - It is simple, ordinary, and confidential.
  - It is loaded with meaning.
  - It looks beyond sorrow to glory.
  "Now that My work is finished, grant Me the desire of My heart, and glorify Me. 'Glorify Me.' In other words, 'take Me to be with You.'"
- The First Reason: "That the Son may glorify Thee."
  "You sent Me into the world to save sinners. Until now, I have constantly used My time to seek and save the lost and give eternal life to those who want to receive it. But the time has come when this work can best be carried on by My being lifted

up. Therefore, exalt Me to Your throne, that from there, as a Prince and Savior, I may dispense the blessings of salvation."
- It involves all mankind.
- It includes His sheep.
- It defines eternal life.
  - An addition by John?
    or
  - An appropriate element.
- It identifies Jesus.
  - An addition by John?
    or
  - An appropriate element.
- The Second Reason: "I have finished the work."

Jesus Prays for His Disciples

- A Description of the Apostles.
  - They were good when He got them.
  - They had maintained their character.
  - They were true believers in Him.
"Jesus prays for them as the precious fruits of His life-long labor, the hope for the future, the founders of the Church, the Noah's ark of the Christian faith, the missionaries who will carry the truth to the whole world."
- Reasons for Granting His Request.
  - It is Your business and Your interest to take care of them.
  - I am no more in the world to take care of them.
- Petitions for the Apostles.
  - That they may be kept in the truth.
  - That they may love one another.
"Truth is the badge which separates His Church from the world. Love is the bond which unites believers of the truth into a holy fellowship which bears witness to the truth."
  - That they may be sanctified in the truth.

Jesus Prays for the Church

- Those Who Would Believe.
  - Through the words of the Apostles.
  - Through the writings of the Apostles.
- Petitions for Believers.
  - That they may be kept in the truth.
  - That they may be sanctified in the truth.
  - That they may be one.

Questions

1. From Jesus' prayer, what do we learn about His mission in life, His use of time, His willingness to sacrifice everything for the glory of His father?
2. Is your mission in life clear to you?
3. When Jesus prayed "Glorify Me," He was expressing His desire to be with the Father. Do you ever long to leave this world and be in the presence of God?
4. Jesus' highest objective was to glorify His Father. Is this your highest objective in life? What competing objectives hinder you from seeking His glory above all else?
5. Jesus acknowledged that He had finished the work the Father had entrusted to Him. What about you? Are you seeking to live a life of obedience so you may receive His praise and reward?
6. Do you understand the Principle of Concentration—focusing on a few who subsequently impact the world? At this point in your own spiritual development, are you committed to discipling a few other people as you have been discipled?
7. Why is it so necessary and important that you faithfully pray for those you are discipling?
8. Explain what is meant by the phrase, "the weight of the Apostles' cross was the measure of their influence."
9. Jesus sacrificed much as He trained the Twelve. Are you committed to doing whatever it takes to expand the kingdom of God by training a few?
10. What can you do to promote the unity of God's people?

11. Are you confident that God will "keep" you in His care until the end?

THE TRAINING OF THE TWELVE
The Sheep Scattered:
44. All the Disciples Left Him and Fled

Scripture

Matthew 26:36-41,55,56,69-75; John 18:15-18

Background

- The Watch.
  - Peter.
  - James.
  - John.
  "The best of the disciples—the three who were the most reliable and selected by Jesus to keep Him company in the Garden of Gethsemane—totally failed to provide the service that was expected of them."
- The Proceedings.
  - Peter.
  - John.
  "And finally, one of them who thought he was bolder than his brothers not only left Him, but denied his beloved Master, declaring with an oath, 'I do not know the man!'"

"The conduct of the disciples at this crisis in their history was so weak and unmanly. Naturally, two questions arise: 1) 'How should they have acted?' and 2) 'Why did they act as they did?'"

How Should They Have Acted?

- What Were Their Options?
  - To run away.
  - To offer resistance.
  - To trust and believe.

- Resisting.
  - Buying swords. Luke 22:35-36
    "Equip yourselves with shoes, purse, and knapsack. Above all, make sure you have your swords and war-like courage."
  - Having swords. Luke 22:38
    "Two swords. Actually they *are* enough, but only for the one who does not intend to fight at all. What were two swords for twelve men against a hundred offensive weapons? The very thought of fighting in those circumstances was absurd."
  - Using the sword. John 18:10-11
    "Though he proved himself to be a coward later among the servants and maids, he was no such coward in the garden."
  "But He did not choose this way, for to overpower His enemies would be to defeat His own purpose in coming to the world. And that purpose was to conquer, not by physical force, but by truth and love and godlike patience…"
- Believing.
  - They were to go on their way. John 18:8
    - Some may have followed.
    - Some may have retired.
  - They were to take care of their lives.
    - They were not needed as a sacrifice.
    - They were needed to declare it.

"They fled in unbelief and despair as men whose hope was blasted."

Why Did the Disciples Act as They Did?

- It Was Anticipated.
  - Jesus predicted it. Matthew 26:31
  - Jesus described it. Matthew 26:41
  "But what do we mean by the weakness of the flesh? Instinctively loving life, dreading danger, fearing man? No. … Their spiritual character at this time was deficient in certain

areas which typically give steadiness to the good impulses of the heart, and mastery over the weaknesses of human nature."

- Character Deficiencies.
  - Forethought.
    - They were asleep.
    - They were surprised.
  - Clear perceptions of truth.
    - They believed in the Messiah.
    - They denied the cross.
  - Ignorance.
    - They believed themselves courageous.
    - They did not know their weaknesses.
  - Experience.
    - This was their first real combat.
    - Other trials were basic training.

"These observations help us understand how it happened that the little flock was scattered when Jesus their shepherd was arrested. The explanation is really proof that the disciples were sheep, not ready to shepherd people."

Questions

1. Can you identify the types of pressures that would cause you to "cave in"—to give up the Christ-like principles you have embraced?

2. The real issue surrounding the disciples' flight from the Garden of Gethsemane was their *lack of faith*. They did not believe God would keep them safe nor did they think everything would turn out right in the end. What about you? Do you implicitly trust the Lord with your whole life?

3. Bruce identifies four missing elements in the character of the disciples that caused them to flee. They are: forethought (they had no idea about what was coming, even though Jesus had given them many hints); clear perceptions of truth (they did not understand the doctrine of Christ); self-knowledge (they did not know their own weaknesses); and the discipline of

experience (they were inexperienced, not veteran). Are any (or all) of these missing in your own life?

4. What needs to take place in the inner core of your being so that you can faithfully follow Christ—to stand boldly in His name—irrespective of the pressure, opposition, risk, or threats?

THE TRAINING OF THE TWELVE
The Sheep Scattered:
45. Sifted as Wheat

Scripture

Luke 22:31,32

Background

- The Setting.
  - The Last Supper.
  - The High Priestly Prayer.
  - The Warning.
- The Warning.
  - Intended directly for Peter.
  - Intended indirectly for all disciples.

"'Satan,' says Jesus 'has demanded permission to sift you' (plural, not singular)—you, Simon and also all of your brothers with you."

A Time for Sifting

- Satan, the Accuser.
  - Skeptical of their faith.
  - Intended to break them.
- Two Crises.
  - After feeding the 5000. John 6
    - Wheat. The disciples.
    - Chaff. The multitudes.
  - After the arrest.
    - Wheat.
      - The devoted, chivalrous, heroic, rock-like Peter.
      - The good in the disciples.
    - Chaff.
      - The vain, self-confident, self-willed, impetuous Peter.

- The vile in the disciples.

"The sifting [at the arrest] is not between man and man, but between the good and the bad, the precious and the vile, *in the same man*."
- The Crises Contrasted.
  - After feeding the 5000.
    - The multitude left.
    - Jesus remained.
  - After the Arrest.
    - The disciples remained
    - Jesus left.

"The following two thoughts summarize the difference between the two 'siftings': 'Christ and us against the world,' and 'Christ in the hands of the world, and we are left all alone.' The results of the sifting process were also different. In the first one, it caused a separation to occur between those who were sincere and those who were insincere. In the final one, it exposed weakness even in those who were sincere."

The Sifting: Dangerous, but not Deadly

- Jesus' View.
  - It would not be deadly.
  - It was certainly dangerous.

  "The disciples demonstrated that they were weak, but not wicked."
- Peter's Failure.

  "We see it [Peter's failure] as a sobering illustration of how close the best men may be brought to the worst."
  - Peter's strategy.
    - He disguised himself.
    - He denied Jesus.
  - Abraham's deceit.
    - He disguised himself.
    - He denied the power of God.

"Peter's act was not less corrupt and selfish, but it was also not more. Both were acts of weakness rather than of wickedness. ... Even those who act like a hero on great occasions will, at other times, act in an unworthy manner."
- Our failures.
  - We have opportunities to speak.
  - We say, "I don't know the Man."
- Peter vs. Judas.
  - Peter was, at heart, a child of God.
  - Peter was kept from falling by special grace.
  - Judas, at the core of his being, was a child of Satan.

"Special grace was given to him [Peter] in order to melt his heart, overwhelm him with an abundance of grief, and cause him to weep out his soul in tears. The wonderful result was produced, not by his piety or goodness of heart, but by God's Spirit and God's providence working toward that end."

Spiritual Benefits of Sifting

- Good from Bad.
  - Strength in grace.
  - Capable of helping.

"Falls, when corrected, can become stepping-stones to Christian virtue. ... People who have erred, and who take their sins seriously, are prone to let their hearts be consumed with their past and waste their time thinking about it. Christ assigns them work to do that is more profitable."
- Peter's Example.
  - Peter's old self.
    - Self-reliant.
    - Arrogant.
  - Peter's new self.
    - Christ-reliant.
    - Obedient.

Questions

1. Have you ever experienced a sifting in which the good and bad in you were searched by the Holy Spirit and your weaknesses exposed?
2. A large part of winning the moral and spiritual battle each day is understanding our weaknesses and asking the Lord to strengthen us in those areas. Do you know yourself well enough to identify your weaknesses? If so, what are some of them?
3. A.B. Bruce says that "with faith, no how uninformed or badly informed, you can overcome the world. Without the kind of faith that consciously places God right beside you, you have no chance." What is the condition of your faith today?
4. Can you remember a time when you denied Christ and were unwilling to be identified with Jesus? Have you changed?
5. How have you seen one of your failures turned into good?

THE TRAINING OF THE TWELVE
The Sheep Scattered:
46. Peter and John

Scripture

John 18:15-18; 19:25-27

Background

- The Setting.
  - The arrest.
  - The interview.
  - The eleven.
- The Witnesses.
  - Peter followed at a distance.
  - John followed with privilege.
- The Association.
  - Before the Ascension.
    - Checking the tomb.
    - Fishing in Galilee.
    - Following Jesus.
  - After the Ascension.
    - In the Temple.
    - Before the rulers.
- The Men.
  - Similarities.
    - Forceful personalities.
    - Daring temperaments.
    - Devoted loyalties.
  - Contrasts.
    - Peter was action-oriented; John was thoughtful.
    - Peter was a natural leader; John was a follower.
    - Peter was the hero; John admired heroism.

Peter and John's Motives and Actions

- Motives.
  - Their love for Jesus.
  - Their concern for His safety.
- Actions.
  - John—Faithful.
    - Witnessed the proceedings.
    - Witnessed the crucifixion.
  - Peter—Failure.
    - Denied Jesus in the courtyard.
    - AWOL at the crucifixion.

"John had the advantage of having a friend in the court. … On the other hand, Peter had no friends in the court. … His untimely courage in the garden helped make him a coward in the yard outside the palace."

Peter and John: The Key Differences

"Peter's temperament opened him up to temptation. John's, however, was a protection against temptation."
- Temperament Differences.
  - Peter.
    - Frank and extroverted.
    - Befriended everyone
  - John.
    - Dignified and reserved.
    - Established boundaries.
- Behavior Differences.
  - Peter—Confronted by servants.
    - Too frank, too open.
    - Too sensitive to public opinion.
  - John—Confronted by servants.
    - Remains quiet.
    - Remains removed.

"Peter's weakness was to be found in his tendency to be friendly with everyone, but without discernment. John, on the other hand, was not in any danger of being on friendly terms with each and every person."

- Behavior Alterations.
  - Peter.
    - Concentration.
    - Discrimination.
  - John.
    - Expansion.
    - Magnanimity.

Questions

1. You have seen how Peter and John were close friends. Describe a close friendship you have with another person. How are the two of you similar? Different? What does this relationship mean to you?

2. As for Peter and John, the motive for our behavior ought to be our deep love for Jesus. Perhaps this would be a good time for you to review the passage found in Revelation 2:4,5, which says, *"But I have this against you, that you have left your first love. Remember therefore where you have fallen, and repent and do the good deeds you did at first; or else I am coming to you and will remove your lampstand—unless you repent."* Have you left your first love? If so, will you return to Him?

3. We have noted the contrasts in Peter and John and the similarities. God has created us all as unique individuals. Would you say you have a good grasp of how God made you, including areas where you may have a greater propensity to fail? What safeguards can you build into your life that would prevent you from succumbing to your most prevalent temptations?

4. Peter "would only learn wisdom by bitter experience." What lessons have you learned through the bitter experiences you have faced?

5. A.B. Bruce addresses a principle that is missed by far too many Christians: *growth in grace may be different for different Christians*. This means husbands will grow differently than their wives; children will grow differently than adults and vice versa. Each person is at a different point on their spiritual journey. Is it easy or difficult for you to allow the Lord to work in another person's life *as He wills and when He wills*? Do you attempt to control (in any way) the spiritual life of a family member? A relative? A friend or neighbor? An employee? If so, how can you change?

6. Peter's fall is a lesson for us all "who do not seek the counsel of God or regard the counsel that is given. They try to accomplish things way beyond their strength." Specifically, what can you do when you are faced with important decisions, temptations, circumstances, etc., to ensure that you do not fall?

THE TRAINING OF THE TWELVE
The Shepherd Restored:
47. Too Good News To Be True

Scripture

Matthew 28:17; Mark 16:11-15; Luke 24:11,13-22,36-42; John 20:20,24-29

Background

- The Setting.
  - After the crucifixion.
  - After the resurrection.
- The Disciples.
  - Their expected mindset.
    - Oh happy day!
    - Unbelievable joy.
    - Eager anticipation.
  - Their actual mindset.
    - Incredible grief.
    - Dashed hopes.

"But their lives are an admirable example to all Christians on how to act when trouble, rebuke, and blasphemy come, or when the cause of Christ seems lost, and the powers of darkness have everything going their own way (for the moment). Though faith is overshadowed and hope extinguished, let the heart always be loyal to its true Lord!"

Responses To Incredible News

- In General.
  - Reaction to the reports.
    - They refused to believe. Mark 16:11
    - They did not believe. Mark 16:13
    - It seemed like nonsense. Luke 24:11

"Their despair after their Lord's crucifixion provides great weight to the testimony given by them about the *fact* of the resurrection. Men who were in this frame of mind were not likely to believe in the resurrection unless it could not be reasonably *disbelieved*."
- Reaction to the appearances.
  - Their hearts were burning. Luke 24:32
  - They thought He was a spirit. Luke 24:37
  - Mary thought He was the gardener. John 20:15
  - Some doubted, others worshipped. Matthew 28:17
- In Particular.
  - The Disciples. John 20:19-23
    - Rejoiced when they saw Him.
    - Received the Holy Spirit.
  - Thomas. John 20:24-29
    - Would not believe without proof.
    - Confessed Him as Lord and God.

"Every one of them approached these appearances with skepticism and went to a lot of trouble to satisfy themselves that what they were seeing was not a ghostly apparition but a living man—the same Man who had died on the cross."

The Theft Theory

"How was the empty tomb supposed to be explained? Mary Magdalene's theory that someone had carried off the corpse would not seem to be all that improbable."
- The Theory.
  - The disciples came at night.
  - The guards were sleeping.
  - The disciples stole the body.
- The Contradictions.
  - Precautions.
    - The sealed tomb.
    - The posted guards.

- Perpetrators?
  - The disciples' state of mind.
  - The disciples' consciences.
  - The disciples' character.

"Did they have any interest in propagating a belief that they did not entertain for themselves? ... They could be convinced that Christ had to die only by His dying, that He would rise only by His rising, that His kingdom was not to be of this world, only by the outpouring of the Spirit at Pentecost..."

Apostolic Preaching

"In their apostolic preaching, they attached supreme importance to the fact of Christ's resurrection and it is our responsibility to do the same."
- The Apostle Paul. 1 Corinthians 15:14
- The Eleven. Martyrs but one.

Questions

1. Are you convinced that the resurrection is a well-attested historical fact? Do you personally believe it happened as recorded in the gospel record?
2. What are some of the implications for you personally if you accept as fact the resurrection of Jesus?
3. The Apostles knew they had to bear witness of such an important event as the resurrection—they knew it was true and they could do nothing less than declare it to the unbelieving world irrespective of the personal cost to them. Is this your passion as well?
4. To this point in your spiritual pilgrimage, have you had the privilege of introducing someone to Christ? If not, what do you think you need to do in order to move up to the front lines as one of His faithful witnesses?

THE TRAINING OF THE TWELVE
The Shepherd Restored:
48. The Eyes of the Disciples Opened

Scripture

Mark 16:14; Luke 24:25-32; John 20:20,20-23; 1 Corinthians 15:5-8

Background

In all, Scripture records nine post-resurrection appearances of Jesus:

1. Mary Magdalene and other women.
   Matthew 28:8-10, John 20:11-18, Mark 16:9-10
2. Peter.
   Luke 24:34, 1 Corinthians 15:5
3. The disciples on the road to Emmaus.
   Luke 24:13-32, Mark 16:12
4. The disciples except Thomas.
   Luke 24:36-43, John 20:19-25
5. The disciples including Thomas.
   Mark 16:14, John 20:26-29
6. Seven disciples at the Sea of Galilee.
   John 21:1-24
7. Eleven disciples on a mountain in Galilee.
   Matthew 28:18-20
8. The Ascension.
   Mark 16:19, Luke 24:44-53, Acts 1:3-12
9. Paul on the road to Damascus. Acts 22:6-10, 1 Corinthians 15:8

Four of the Post Resurrection Appearances

Bruce examines four of the post resurrection appearances in this lesson: Mary Magdalene, Peter, the disciples on the road to Emmaus, and the disciples without Thomas.

- Mary Magdalene. Bruce thinks that her sorrow and tears upon discovering the empty grave moved Jesus to her side to comfort her.
  - Jesus. "Why are you weeping? Whom do you seek?"
  - Mary. "Sir, if you have carried Him away... I will take Him."
- Peter. Bruce correctly states that we have no details of this meeting, but he does speculate about its nature.
  - Jesus knew Peter's grief over his failure.
  - He desired to tell Peter he was forgiven.
- The Road to Emmaus. The two disciples walking to Emmaus shifted between despair and hope.
  - They were devastated when they thought of the crucifixion.
  - They wondered if it were possible that He had risen again.
- The Ten. When Jesus appeared to the ten, they were terrified, thinking they were seeing a spirit—the ghost of the crucified One. Jesus:
  - Quiets their fears and convinces them it is He Himself.
  - Explains to them the true nature of the Messiah.

With typical insight, Bruce notes that the process of revelation Jesus uses for "the two" and "the ten" are exactly opposite.

- The Two.
  - He speaks to their minds.
  - He opens their eyes.
- The Ten.
  - He opens their eyes to the facts.
  - He then speaks to their minds.

The important conclusion from this is these are exactly the ways individuals are brought to faith. And we need to be sensitive to this fact when we share with others.

161

The Impact of Jesus' Exposition of Scripture

Did the disciples gain enough light from these expositions that they would need no further illumination? Had Jesus already fulfilled the work of the Holy Spirit and led the disciples into all truth?

- The opening of their understanding which took place at this time did not, by any means, amount to a full spiritual enlightenment in Christian doctrine.
- The difference between the disciples' frame of mind after Jesus explained the law to them and after the Holy Spirit came was vast:
  - Before Pentecost, they only knew the basics of the doctrine of Jesus—it was as if a single ray of light came into their minds.
  - When they matured, they were thoroughly initiated into the Mystery of the Gospel—the daylight of truth flooded their souls.

"Their hearts were set on fire when they had become very dry and withered—hopeless, sick and weary because of their sorrow and disappointment. For this is the way it always is: the fuel must be dry in order for the spark to set it on fire. ... Their worldly ambition prevented them from learning the spirituality of Christ's kingdom, and their pride blinded them to the glory of the cross."

Questions

1. The two on the road to Emmaus could not see Jesus because their hearts were full of sorrow. What keeps you from seeing Jesus as he really is?
2. Jesus used the Old Testament to demonstrate that His life was a fulfillment of its prophecies about the Messiah. Have you perhaps unwittingly become only a "New Testament Christian"? As one person put it, "If I only read and study the New Testament, I am only prepared to use a single-edged dagger. But when I read and study the Old and New Testaments, I have in my hands a two-edged sword" (Hebrews

4:12). How have you neglected the study of the whole Bible? Identify the issues which keep you from studying all of God's revelation. Then ask the Lord to help you overcome the barriers that keep you from it.

3. Some come to Christ by first considering the historical facts of His life, death and resurrection. Others cannot see the facts until the eyes of their heart are illumined to see the "beauty and the worthiness of the truth as it is in Jesus." How does this truth affect the way you do evangelism?

4. What is the role of the Holy Spirit in opening our eyes to see with the heart?

5. Why is it important for the heart to become dry as a prelude to revival?

6. What key instrument does Bruce say can dry out the heart?

THE TRAINING OF THE TWELVE
The Shepherd Restored:
49. The Doubt of Thomas

Scripture

John 20:24-29

Background

- The Setting.
  - After the crucifixion.
  - After the resurrection.
- The Disciple Thomas.
  - His Absence.
    - What was his reason?
    - Was he still grieving?
  - His Skepticism.
    - A member of the Sadducees?
    - His melancholy temperament. John 11:16
    - His demand for proof.

"He would not be satisfied with the testimony of his brothers. He must have credible evidence for himself—not that he doubted their truthfulness. But he could not get rid of the suspicion that what they had seen was only a ghost. He felt that their eyes had been deceived."

- Modern Doubters.
  - Trouble believing in the supernatural.
  - Trouble accepting the consequences.
    - Everlasting shame.
    - Everlasting contempt
  - Sincere doubt.

"But the risen Lord makes a second appearance for his special benefit and offers him the proof he needed. ... There may be something of a rebuke here, but there is more compassion than anything else. Jesus speaks to a sincere disciple whose faith is weak, and not to one who has an evil heart that is filled with unbelief."

Thomas' Faith

- The Proof.
  - Did Thomas actually mean what he said?
    - It was an off-the-cuff comment.
    - It reflected his melancholy.
  - Did Thomas actually inspect the wounds?
    - The narrative does not suggest this.
    - His response is based on sight.
    - It is inconsistent with his nature.

"And after he has seen the ugly wounds and heard Jesus' kind words, he is ashamed of his rash, reckless speech to his brothers. Overcome with joy and tears, he exclaims, 'My Lord and my God.'"

- The Confession.
  - Most advanced of the Twelve.
    - "The Christ the Son of the Living God." Peter
    - "My Lord and my God." Thomas
  - The fullest and strongest belief.
    - Convinced doubters are sound.
    - Convinced doubters are enthusiastic.
    - Convinced doubters are devoted.
  - The Socinian explanation. [denial of Christ's deity]
    - A natural interpretation.
    - An expression of astonishment.

"This interpretation is absolutely desperate. It disregards the text itself. When Thomas spoke these words, he was answering and speaking to Jesus. The interpretation also forces a man who is bursting with emotion to speak coldly."

The Meaning of Thomas' Profession

- The First phrase. "My Lord."
  - Affirms Jesus is alive.
  - Recognizes Jesus as Master.
- The Second phrase. "My God."
  - Acknowledges Christ's divinity.
  - Affirms that death is defeated.

"When he demanded the physical evidence, he had been standing on a low platform of faith. Now he has moved to a higher platform, where he feels this kind of evidence is unnecessary."

Believing Without Seeing

"But what does Jesus mean when He pronounces a beatitude or blessing on those who do not see, and yet believe?"
- He does not commend those who believe without making *any* inquiry.
- He does not imply that joy goes only to those who never doubt.

"He wants those who must believe without seeing to understand that they do not have any reason to envy those who had an opportunity to see and then believed only after they saw. ... We may begin, in our weakness, by being Thomases, clinging eagerly to every piece of external evidence in order to save ourselves from drowning. But, as we grow, we can end up with a faith that *almost* amounts to sight, rejoicing in Jesus as our Lord and God, with joy unspeakable and full of glory."

Questions

1. Thomas missed a good sermon because he wasn't where he should have been. A.B. Bruce states that we cannot ever know when good things are going to come to us. But we can "be where we ought to be and do what we ought to do." That is the

only way to ensure that we get them. Give an example of the following from your life:

   a. You were in the wrong place at the wrong time?

   b. You missed a golden opportunity because you were somewhere else at the time.

   c. You were doing something you should not have been doing, and you suffered some consequences as a result.

   d. You procrastinated and missed something special.

2. Being where we ought to be and doing what we ought to be doing is another way of describing obedience. Are you seeking to live a life of obedience to Christ?

3. Describe your own temperament. For you is the cup generally "half full" or "half empty"?

4. Do you struggle with doubt over any of the basic tenants of the Christian faith (for example, the virgin birth, the deity and humanity of Christ, the Trinity, the inspiration and inerrancy of Scripture, salvation by grace through faith)? How have you sought to deal with these doubts?

5. At this time in your life, do you need help with any of your doubts?

THE TRAINING OF THE TWELVE
The Under-Shepherds Admonished:
50. Pastoral Duty

Scripture

John 21:15-17

Background

- The Setting.
    - After appearing to the women.
    - After appearing to Peter.
    - After appearing to the two on the road.
    - After appearing to the disciples.
    - After appearing to the disciples and Thomas.
- The Expedition.
    - To get food.
    - A return.
        - To old habits.
        - To familiar surroundings.
    - A vacation.
        - Fatigued by sorrow.
        - Surprised by Jesus.
- Their Mindset.
    - Life as Fishermen.
    "Here in our native province of Galilee, we can pursue our old calling. We can think, believe, and act as we please. And we will live in obscurity and be protected from all danger. We will be delightfully free and independent in this rustic life by the shores of the Sea."
    - Life as Apostles.
    "We will be carrying a heavy burden of responsibility and will be obligated to constantly think about others, not ourselves. There is a possibility that we could have our personal liberty taken away from us. In fact, we may lose our lives."

"If the simple life they left behind was so happy, why did they leave it? … Life is more than food. The kingdom of God is man's primary purpose."

Jesus Awakens The Seven Disciples

- Instructions to the Seven.
  - How to catch fish.
    - "Fishers of men."
    - Apostolic work.
  - Invitation to eat.
    - Concerns of the world, vs.
    - Undivided service.
- Instructions to Peter.
  - Reminder of failures.
    - The timing—as they were eating (also Last Supper)
    - The name—not Peter, but Simon son of Jonas.
    - The question asked three times—"Do you love Me?"
    - The comparison in the question—"more than these?" Matthew 26:33
    - The admonition—"Tend My lambs." Matthew 26:31
    "The idea suggested [by Jesus' responses is] that the man who has fallen the most deeply and learned the most thoroughly what his own weaknesses are is, or ought to be, the best qualified person for strengthening those who are weak—for feeding the lambs."
  - Restoration as an Apostle?
    "We are not able to agree with those who maintain that, during this meeting, Jesus formally restored the erring disciple to his position as an Apostle."
    - Peter's behavior on seeing Jesus.
    - Jesus' remonstrances of Peter.

Peter's Recall

"This encounter is not about Peter being restored to a position he had forfeited. It is his recall to a more solemn understanding of his high calling."

- The motivation for shepherds.
  - My forgiveness, your gratitude.
  - Because your brothers need it.
  - Out of devotion to Me.
- The model for shepherds.
  - Peter, the undisciplined fisherman, or
  - Peter, the martyred Apostle.

  "The young, playful, determined fisherman went here and there and did just as he pleased; the old saintly Apostle, meek as a lamb, stretched forth his arms to be bound for martyrdom. What a moving contrast! ... Who, therefore, could better illustrate man's need for shepherding?"
- The power for shepherds.

Shepherds or Sheep

"We must add, that all who are motivated by the spirit of love for the Redeemer will either be shepherds or sheep."

- Shepherds. Care for the souls of others.
- Sheep.
  - Cared for by shepherds.
  - Too self-willed to be led.

Evidence of Peter's Readiness

- Obvious humility—no more comparisons.
- Godly sorrow—not anger or shame.

Questions

1. Are you currently living a life of selfishness—thinking about yourself, doing for yourself—or a life of service to others?
2. Peter was recalled to "a more solemn understanding of his high calling." Did you ever serve Christ with all your heart and then, at some point in time, the fire within grew dim? Do you need to be recalled? Will you answer the call?
3. Are you a shepherd or a sheep?
4. If a shepherd, who are you leading? If a sheep, who are you following?
5. Do you have a tendency to avoid taking responsibility for the lives of others? If so, how can you change?
6. What do you believe is the main purpose of your existence?

THE TRAINING OF THE TWELVE
The Under-Shepherds Admonished:
51. Pastor Pastorum

Scripture

John 21:19-22

Background

- The Setting.
  - Appearances.
    - To the women.
    - To Peter.
    - To the two on the road.
    - To the disciples.
    - To the disciples and Thomas.
    - To the disciples and Peter.
  - Instructions.
    - Jesus and Peter apart.
    - John at a distance.
- The Conversation.
  - Feed My lambs.
  - Feed My sheep.

"Pastors are not lords over God's people. They are simply servants of Christ, who is the great Head of the Church, and are required to think of His will as their law, and His life as their example."

  - Follow Me.

"If one wants to fulfill his duty as an under-shepherd, he must be a faithful sheep and follow the Chief Shepherd wherever He goes."

- The Question.

"Lord, what about this man [John]?"

  - Is John's fate to be the same as mine, or
  - Will he be exempt because You love him?

"We believe Peter was afraid that John would receive a better and happier outcome in life than him. ... Adversity is hard to bear. But it is hardest when one's personal struggles are compared with the prosperity of a brother who started his career at the same time, and had no better prospects than the person whom he has beaten in the race."

Jesus' Response to Peter's Question

- Some possible replies.
    - John will experience tribulation.
    - Longevity is not the issue.
- Some character concerns.
    - Weakness.
    - Longing for happiness.
    - Sulking over missed pleasures.
- Some attributes for followers.
    - Strengths He desires.
        - To be heroes.
        - Fearless in the face of danger.
        - Patient when fatigued.
        - Without selfish softness.
    - Weaknesses He forbids.
        - Present pain.
        - Smarting from rebuke.
- The Outcomes.
    - John. "It might be said that because of his temperament, John was less exciting than his brother Apostle. He was not as impetuous as Peter, but just as intense. And perhaps his character did not provoke the world to opposition like Peter's did."
    - Peter. "Peter, however, because of his virtues and his weaknesses, was predestined to be the *champion* of the faith, the Luther of the apostolic age. He gave and received the hardest blows and bore the brunt of the battle."

The First Pope?

"He had no intention of making him a pastor of pastors, a shepherd or bishop over his fellow disciples. … Neither Peter nor any other person is able to bear [the burden of being the visible Christ to the Church]."

- The main business of under-shepherds.
    - Not to make others follow Christ, but
    - To follow Him themselves.
- The main business of followers.
    "Each person makes his most effective contribution for everyone's good when he lives his own life by godly principles."

Follow Me

- Peter's Obedience.
    - A fleshly desire for happiness.
    - A desire to be exempt from the cross.
    - Questioning obedience.
- Jesus' Expectation.
    - Following without distraction, murmuring, or envy.
    - Following without weighing consequences.
    - Following with cheerful, exact, habitual obedience.
    - Acknowledging His right to lead as He pleases.
    - Thinking of all His orders as wise; all His arrangements good.
    - Content to serve Him in a little place or a big one.

"This is our duty. It is also our blessing. When we begin to think this way, we will be delivered from all concern about consequences, from ambitious thoughts about our responsibilities, from imaginary hurts, from envy, worry, and the restlessness of self-will."

Questions

1. Are you prepared and committed to follow Jesus wherever He leads, irrespective of the personal consequences?
2. Do you have a tendency to compare yourself with other believers as Peter did with John? Can you let go and leave them in the Lord's hands?
3. A.B. Bruce says God wants "all of His followers to be heroes." What does he mean by this? Are you one of his heroes?
4. Are you currently following Christ by seeking to live your life according to godly principles? If not, are you willing to submit to His Lordship?
5. How much has the goal of "being happy" affected and guided your life?
6. Your great concern in life ought to be "that God be glorified." Can you say that this is the driving force of your life even over personal peace and happiness?

THE TRAINING OF THE TWELVE
52. Power From On High

Scripture

Matthew 28:18-20; Mark 16:15; Luke 24:47-53; Acts 1:1-8

Background

- The Setting.
  - Final Instructions.
    - Apostolic duties.
    - Apostolic power.
  - The Audience. Acts 1:14
    - The disciples.
    - The women.
    - Jesus' brothers.

  "Before His death, Jesus was like a parent speaking His last words of counsel and comfort to His sorrowing children. After His resurrection, He was 'like a man, away on a journey, who upon leaving his house and putting his slaves in charge, assigning to each one his task, also commanded the doorkeeper to stay on the alert (Mark 13:34).'"

- The Sequence.
  - The Great Commission.
    - Matthew 28:16-20 (Galilee).
    - Mark 16:14-15 (Jerusalem).
    - Luke 24:47-53 (Jerusalem).
  - The Holy Spirit.
    - Waiting. Luke 24:49
    - Witnessing. Acts 1:8
  - The Ascension.
    - Jerusalem. Luke 24:50-51
    - Bethany. Acts 1:9-11

  "In essence, this is what He was saying, 'I have all power in heaven and jurisdiction over all the earth. You go, therefore, into all the world and make disciples of all the nations. Do not doubt for a moment that all spiritual influences and all providential means will be provided for you so you can accomplish the great errand on which I am sending you.'"

The Ascension

"The way in which He ascended was most gracious and kind toward those He left behind."
- His Manner.
  - His face looked downward.
  - His voice was blessing them.
- Their Reaction.
  - They were amazed.
  - They were joyful.
  - They worshipped.

"We are unable to comment on that miraculous moment when our High Priest passed through the veil into the celestial sanctuary. ... It cannot be explained."

The Great Commission

- Divinely Inspired.
  - Gigantic in scope.
  - Motivated by love.
- Strategically Conceived.
  - Jerusalem.
    "Why begin in Jerusalem? Because Jerusalem sinners are the ones who most need to repent and be forgiven."
  - Judea and Samaria.
  - The world.

"What a commission for poor Galilean fishermen to receive! What a burden of responsibility to lay on the shoulders of any poor mortal! Who is adequate for these things?"

Power from on High

"The power He was talking about was not primarily a power to perform miracles."

- The Mission of the Comforter.
  - Enlightenment of their minds.
  - The enlargement of their hearts.
  - The sanctification of their talents.
  - The transformation of their character.
- The Manifestation of the Comforter.

  "The power, therefore, was a spiritual power, not a magical power. It was an inspiration, not a possession. ... It was to manifest itself as a spirit of love and of a sound mind."
  - They were more rational.
  - They were sober minded.
  - They were calm expositors of truth.

"They were to be less like their past selves and more like their Master—no longer ignorant, childish, weak, carnal, but initiated into the mysteries of the kingdom, and habitually under the guidance of the Spirit of grace and holiness."

Questions

1. How are you currently involved in helping to fulfill the great commission?
2. Do you know how to appropriate the power of the Holy Spirit in order to "make disciples of all the nations?"
3. Where is your Jerusalem? In other words, where is the place the Lord would have you begin sharing the Gospel with others?
4. In order for you to be effective as a witness, you must receive many things from the Holy Spirit including, "the enlightenment of your mind, the enlargement of your heart, the sanctification of your talent, and the transformation of your character." Meditate on each of these and ask the Lord to show you anything that may be hindering your effectiveness as His witness.

THE TRAINING OF THE TWELVE
53. Waiting

Scripture

Acts 1:1-8

Background

- The Setting.
  - After the Ascension.
    - The believers wait as commanded,
    - In the upper room in Jerusalem.
  - The Audience. Acts 1:14
    - The disciples.
    - Jesus' mother and brothers.
    - The women.
    - Others.
- The Crisis.
  - Their history.
    - The dreary, bleak time is ended.
      - Mental confusion is diffusing.
      - Despairing sorrow is now joy.
    - Their vague notion of the future,
      - Will be made understandable.
      - Great things will be revealed.
  - Their future.
    - They will experience great illumination.
      - The Spirit of Truth is coming.
      - The morning star is about to rise.
    - They will be endowed with:
      - The ability to speak.
      - A changed character.
    - When others hear them.
      - They will be amazed,
      - Hearing native tongues.
- How Do They Wait?
  - They prayed for:
    - The power of the Holy Spirit.

179

- ▪ Additional light on Scripture.
- ▪ The coming of the Kingdom.
- They selected a replacement.
- They read the Scriptures.
  - ▪ Psalm 16.
  - ▪ Psalm 109.
  - [Used in Peter's Pentecost sermon.]
- They discussed spiritual matters.
  - ▪ Asking questions.
  - ▪ Giving answers.

Pentecost

- The Setting.
  - Time.
    - ▪ After the ascension. Acts 1:3
    - ▪ The day of Pentecost. Acts 2:1
  - Location. Jerusalem.
  - Characters.
    - ▪ Peter.
    - ▪ Jesus' followers.
    - ▪ The ten.
    - ▪ Crowds.
- The Arrival of the Holy Spirit.
  - Physical manifestations.
    - ▪ Like a rushing, mighty wind.
    - ▪ Cloven tongues like fire.
  - Tangible outcomes.
    - ▪ The disciples were filled.
    - ▪ They spoke in tongues.
    - ▪ They received power.
- Misconceptions About the Kingdom.
  - They assumed Christ would reign on earth.
    - ▪ His Kingdom is not of this world.
    - ▪ His citizens believe the truth.
  - They assumed Christ would restore Israel.
    - ▪ He called them to the world.
    - ▪ Jerusalem, Judea, Samaria…

- They assumed His Kingdom was political.
  - The power of the Holy Spirit is,
  - Moral, not political.

The True Nature of the Kingdom

- The Ruler of the Kingdom.
  - The King is omnipresent.
  - The Kingdom is universal.
- The Understanding of the Kingdom Revealed.
  - At the ascension.
  - At Pentecost.
  - At the conversion of:
    - Samaritans.
    - And Gentiles.

A Final Word

- Jesus gave the disciples lessons on:
  - The nature of the Kingdom.
  - Prayer.
  - Religious liberty/the nature of holiness.
  - His own Person and claims.
  - The doctrine of the cross; importance of His death.
  - Humility and similar virtues.
  - Christian character required of disciples.
  - The doctrine of self-sacrifice.
  - The dangers of Pharisaism and Sadduceeism.
  - The mission of the Comforter.
- The disciples were transformed.
  - Their minds were enlightened.
  - They were endowed with love.
  - They were serious about their job.
  - They were delivered from superstitions.
  - They were emancipated from:
    - Customs.
    - Traditions.

- Commandments of men.
- Their hearts had been cleansed.

"They were men who were made of excellent moral stuff. So it shouldn't surprise us that since they were with Jesus so long, they would prove to be exceptionally good and noble men when they came before the world as leaders of a great movement, and were called on to carry out their responsibilities."

Questions

1. The 120 believers in the upper room waited until they received the promised power from the Holy Spirit. Is your practice to wrestle and wait on God in prayer for His power to minister in his name…or do you attempt to minister in your own strength, in the power of the flesh?
2. Have you learned to pray without giving up?
3. After studying the Word of God with the help of this magnificent work by A.B. Bruce, can you say you now have a clear understanding of the Kingdom of God? If so, take a few minutes to write down some of the characteristics of His Kingdom.
4. "The little flock grew greatly, not by might, nor by the power of this world, but by God's Spirit." Can you now personalize this truth and, by faith, trust God to use you in the lives of a small group of people who need you to disciple them? When will you begin?
5. How has your life changed since you began this study about Jesus and the Twelve?

Ministries of mercy
the call of the Jer Rodd
Tim keller.

Made in the USA
Lexington, KY
20 September 2015